"I Don't Believe It!"

Memories Of A Detroit Lions Fan

Barry Schumer

Bloomington, IN  Milton Keynes, UK

authorHOUSE™

AuthorHouse™
1663 Liberty Drive, Suite 200
Bloomington, IN 47403
www.authorhouse.com
Phone: 1-800-839-8640

AuthorHouse™ UK Ltd.
500 Avebury Boulevard
Central Milton Keynes, MK9 2BE
www.authorhouse.co.uk
Phone: 08001974150

First published by AuthorHouse 7/28/2006

ISBN: 1-4259-4394-2 (sc)
ISBN: 1-4259-4395-0 (dj)

Library of Congress Control Number: 2006905623

Printed in the United States of America
Bloomington, Indiana

This book is printed on acid-free paper.

I dedicate this book to all of the long-suffering fans of the Detroit Lions, for all the disappointment, frustration and pain that they have experienced year after year after year. We all love this team and the NFL game; however, the losing and mismanagement have been cruel. The months of January through July provide a welcome respite when we can heal and regenerate our hope. I also want to recognize the pain and suffering of our fellow NFL fans of the Arizona Cardinals, New Orleans Saints and Cleveland Browns. The fans of the Jacksonville Jaguars and Houston Texans have suffered too short a time to belong to our special club.

I would like to acknowledge my long suffering Lions buddies, Al, Larry, Jim, Chuck, Ted, Alice, Scott, Ernie, Lawrence, Dave, Chris, Mark, Mike, Steve, Stuart, James and David. Is it possible that the hours and days of analyzing the Lions were all wasted? Are we really giving up on our football team?

I want to thank my wonderful girlfriend Stephanie who always believed in me and this project. To my son Jason and daughter Marissa, you both inspire me daily. Also, I thank my brother Chuck whose encouragement kept me on task. And last, to my mother Vera, who taught our family never to give up. And to the sports radio stations and sports journalists in Detroit – your shows and articles kept us all informed during the traumatic days and years.

Table of Contents

Chapter 1

Two moments in Lions
history never forgotten!

November 8, 1970, my best friend Al and I were watching what would become one of the most memorable moments in Detroit Lions history. I was 15 and Al was 16. Being sports nuts, we followed the four major sports in Detroit with an amazing passion. But our devotion to NFL football and our Lions was unique. The average fan may find it a complicated and difficult game to understand because what appears to be obvious is not. It is a thinking man's game, much like a chess match. I have often compared it to war, led by generals - footballs flying instead of bullets. Of the four major sports, football fields the most players, 22, at the same time - baseball 10-13, basketball 10, hockey 12. Due to how difficult this sport is, and how crucial strategy becomes, the head coach in football is more important than in any other major sport. I believe this is what makes football so special - and why fans' passions are so intense.

Let's get back to that day in 1970. We were at Al's house in Detroit watching what would be the first of many more "I don't believe it's!" concerning our beloved Detroit Lions. The Lions were leading New Orleans 17-16 with a few seconds left on the clock. Tom Dempsey was about to make history, kicking a 63 yard field goal to beat Detroit, ripping our hearts out for the first of many times to come. Attempting a field goal from that distance seemed almost laughable. In fact, it was said that linebacker Alex Karris was laughing so hard that he never got set in his position for the kick. Watching that kick, I remember hearing the thud of the kicker's foot striking the ball and watching it fall incredibly just over the uprights. The Saints won. Al and I looked at each other and, at the same time screamed, "I don't believe it."

Flash forward to December 19, 2004, the Lions vs. the Vikings. That was the game that finally inspired me to write this book. Once again, the expression "I don't believe it!" proved appropriate. In the last minute of the fourth quarter, Joey Harrington led the Lions down the field to score the apparent tying touchdown, that would send the game into overtime. Winning this game was crucial because, after starting the season 4-2, Harrington and the team had suffered a terrible stretch, losing seven of their last eight games. More importantly, they still had a very good chance of making the playoffs (due to how many teams in the NFC were struggling). When they came on the field for the extra point, they seemed to be taking an especially long time with the kick. The holder kept looking back at the kicker to make sure he was ready. At that moment, something strange happened. Maybe because of my 34 years of experience as a fan, I thought to myself, "they are going to miss the extra point". Botched snap, game over – "I don't believe it". One of the radio announcers for Minnesota said "the Lions don't believe they can win". Joey Harrington's lips read "unbelievable".

The year 2004 was a particularly strange one for me as a Lions fan. It was the year I finally "snapped". I was excited about their 4-2 start; I was sure they would go to the playoffs, and the rebuilding program under Millen was beginning to work. We had drafted and developed some great young talent. We felt we had the coach to lead the team into the future. In 2006 the Super Bowl is in Detroit; maybe our Lions will be playing in front of their home crowd! Back to reality.

Chapter 2

Memories of Detroit
sports as a teenager

Al is the radio engineer for the Lions. I remember us being down in his basement as teenagers, and how he was always fooling around with ham radios. After we didn't see each other for about 15 years, I saw Al on TV doing the NBA finals with Michael Jordan. He had headphones on and was the radio engineer for the NBA. I had no idea he had become that successful from his hobby as a teenager. He works the World Series, Super Bowl, College football and basketball championships, the NBA finals, most of the all star games and most of the Detroit major sports teams. He invited me to the national championship game for college football in Miami a few years ago. There was a national sports magazine article written about Al that started with "he has seen more championship games than Michael Jordan and Derrick Jeeter combined". I am proud of my friend for what he has achieved in life. We have become great friends again these past 10 years. We remain passionate about sports, but are mostly great golf buddies.

Al and I were best friends as teenagers. We met when I was 12 years old. There is something unique about a childhood friendship. It stays with you the rest of your life. Al and I would spend hours together centered on sports. I slept over his house quite often on weekends.

During the winter, we would make an ice rink in his back yard. We would wake up at 3am to give it another coat of water. We both loved hockey and grew up watching Gordie Howe at the end of his career. We built a make shift hockey net one year out of two by fours and an old blanket. We would get dressed in all the goalie gear that Al's brother had; when we shot the puck, it would hit the wooden post and the net would collapse. Those were great memories.

When we went to Olympia stadium to see Gordie Howe, Alex Delvecchio, Frank Mahovlich and Micky Redmond, we found a unique way to get into the stadium. We went to almost every home game for a few years, but the ticket prices of $7 were hard to afford. One night, we were looking for tickets outside the stadium, and a guy with a Colombo trench coat calls us over. He says you guys want to get into the game for $2? Just go through that gate with that usher and say "hi Louie." We paid our $2 and the usher let us through with the password. There would be a different password every night. We did this for a year or two, before their operation got busted and we had to buy tickets the old fashioned way. We will never forget our days down at Olympia.

Al and I went to a Tiger game one night and parked far from the stadium to save money. When we came back to the car after the game, we noticed a gang of five or six teens looking suspicious following us. We could sense they were about to jump us so we made a run for the car. I had my shoulder in a sling due to a separation and did the best I could to run. We just got to the car and got in when these kids reached us and began pulling on the doors as we just locked them. Al began beeping the horn which got them to run. Our hearts were in our throats. We were very lucky that night.

❖❖❖

My father died when I was six years old and my mother had significant problems after this. My teenage years were filled with stress and uncertainty. My attachment to friends and sports was an effort to fill the void I felt in my life. Something always seemed to be missing for me. The passion I got from playing and following sports was very important to me. It was a great escape for me. Sport represents a great escape for many people, for many different reasons.

All people, I have found, have different experiences growing up in their families. Some have typical, happy childhoods, raised by fairly normal parents. Many are not as lucky and grow up around multiple stresses and problems. I was actually quite lucky in some ways because I had older siblings that lessoned some of the problems our family faced after our father's death in 1962. As a social worker, I have seen many sad things happen to people and families over 25 years of practice. Death, divorce, alcoholism, child abuse, suicide, medical and mental illness and depression can hit any family. Everyone learns to cope and go on through life the best way they can. We learn our coping strengths from our parents and families. Some people learn to cope with anything life throws their way and are well adjusted, happy people. Others never recover from early trauma and problems, going through life angry, depressed or unhappy.

I have been very lucky in my life. I have learned to cope as a process of facing bad decisions and disasters. I have never had much money, but I do all right. I have survived two divorces and feel I understand myself and relationships better now. I am the best father I know how to be to my 18 and 14 year old son and daughter. I have a wonderful girlfriend who helps me to grow as a person. Sports is simply one of my distractions in life; I take the winning and losing less seriously than I used too, but winning is definitely better. Everyone needs a hobby!

Sport offers a wonderful escape from the pressures of life. Watching or participating are both healthy ways to take a break from life. Golf is the sport I play. As many people know, this can be a rather frustrating endeavor and may not be considered relaxing by many. I have gotten pretty good at the game by learning patience and never giving up. I am a 10 handicap and got my first hole in one this past year. I also enjoy shooting a basketball, although I am not very good at the game because of a bad leg. I have a pretty good shot however and can beat people at horse, three point shooting or best out of 20 foul shots.

Chapter 3

Is there a Lions curse?

In 2004 the Lions fans seem to have finally lost it. I have never seen so much anger and frustration by fans. Some people make it too important; it is "just a game" after all, isn't it? I am worried that fans are about to take things too far as the 2004 season comes to an end. Some fans are a little "disturbed", if you know what I mean. They have terrible tempers. The most dangerous crowd I have ever been in was when I went to see Michigan play Ohio State in Columbus. The fans at the Horseshoe that day were frightening. I thought my life was at risk. Too many people that were drunk; too many people acting like their lives were coming to an end as Ohio State lost that day. I hope that never happens with the Lions at Ford Field.

A few months ago, Al asked me if I wanted to join him in Jacksonville in November of 2004, for a Lions game. We went down and golfed twice before the Sunday game; we got to play the famous 17th hole at the TPC of Sawgrass; the island green par three for the Players Championship. What a great experience. Saturday night I helped Al set up his radio booth for the game. I had the opportunity to go into the Lions locker room as the crew was unloading their equipment. I saw their helmets, pads and shoes lined up in the lockers. Again, it reminded me of soldiers preparing to go to war. After almost 35 years as a fan, here I was in my Lion's locker room on the road. It hit me just how much this team meant to me. The pride I felt of being from Detroit.

People in the United States are all pretty much the same. For the most part, they are friendly people who care about their families, work hard and live life within the "rules." People have pride in the cities they grew up in and live in as adults. The only cities that are a little different are New York and Los Angeles – they are different because of their size, but even in those cities there are great people who are very proud of where they live. There is something that gives people a special feeling when the team from their city wins a championship. It's as though the fan feels like they are a winner. They feel that they are special for at least those few weeks.

Game day saw clouds and 40 mile an hour winds (I was hoping for some Florida sunshine). The Lions were losing 17-0 when I had to leave at the end of the 3rd quarter to catch my plane home. I heard Eddie Drummond's first punt return for a touchdown in the car; when I got to the airport and saw a television, I was amazed to see a 17-17 tie in overtime. Drummond had run another back all the way in the last minute to tie the game. We lost in overtime; the offense never touched the ball.

❖❖❖

I have been a season ticket holder in three stadiums over the years. I have seen games in Tiger Stadium, the Silver dome and now Ford Field. I will recall some of the great times through this book. It has not all been torture, just most of it. As I said, 2004 had been a particularly hard one for me. I was having problems waiting for a great team. There have been times I have told friends that the Lions look like they are playing a different sport than the best teams in the NFL. The games just look different.

I "snapped" again after we blew a 19-7 lead at Minnesota a few weeks ago in December 2004. Adjustments by the coach at halftime are critical in football; we had not done well in this area this season. I

as in a bad state of mind, when I was openly rooting for
na Cardinals to beat the Lions. I had never done that in 34
years of following the team. I was actually disappointed when the
Lions won the game - their only win in 8 games. I knew the pressure
of being a Lion fan was finally starting to get to me. I would often
joke with friends, that being a Lions fan was not good for one's
mental health. Being a social worker, I felt that there should be an
official psychiatric disorder in the DSM-IV referring to the risks and
symptoms of following this team for any extended period of time. I
had become bitter and angry. I felt I had to disconnect emotionally
from this team I have loved. Sometimes you just need to walk away
from a relationship that is bringing you down. I will miss my team,
but hope to be back in the future - I know I will never stop loving
them.

I feel so bad for Mr. Ford and his family who has owned the team since
1964. I'm sure no one wants to bring a Super Bowl title to Detroit
more than him. I hear he is a fantastic person. I am convinced that
this city would celebrate a Super Bowl championship more intensely
than any other for the Tigers, Red Wings or Pistons. The city would
go crazy! It's hard to know what the answer is, but a lot of people
with a lot of experience are working on it. I hope they get it right.
Before I die, I want to watch my Lions win a Super Bowl. OK, maybe
just play in a Super Bowl.

The Lion's won three championships from 1935-1957 and were 6-1
in playoff games. Since 1957, they are 1-9 in playoff games; the only
win that I witnessed was the 38-6 victory over Dallas in 1991. That
was the year we appeared in the NFC championship game. Is that the
closest we will ever be to the Super Bowl? We hope not.

❖❖❖

Before we review the highlights and lowlights since 1970, we want to
address the so called Honolulu blue and silver curse. Does one really
exist? Has this organization had far more bad luck than any other
professional sports team in history? We think the answer might be

yes! Besides finding amazing ways to lose games, the Lions have had an unbelievable amount of personal tragedy on and off the field. I was in the crowd at Tiger Stadium that horrible day October 24th 1971, two days before I turned 16 years old. Chuck Hughes died that day of a heart attack after running a pass route. We remember Dick Butkus signaling to the side lines that something was seriously wrong with Chuck. I remember getting home from the game won by the Bears and finding out he had died. Not many sports fans can say they saw a player die during a game. I came very close to seeing my second Detroit Lion player die on Dec.21st, 1997. One day after I married my second wife, I took my step-son to see the Jets game. The Lions needed the win to make the playoffs, and Barry Sanders was closing in on 2000 yards rushing. The Lion's outstanding linebacker, Reggie Brown did not move after a collision involving his neck. You could tell it was very serious. I thought back to the game with Chuck Hughes. Was I really witnessing the death of a second Lion player 26 years later? We were very worried about that possibility; and were amazed at hearing how close he came to death that day. The work of the trainer and doctor saved his life.

The deaths of Coach Don MCaffery during training camp in 1974. The death of Eric Andelsack in a bizarre incident during the off season. Mike Utley's being paralyzed during a game. I'm not sure if any other professional team has ever had to deal with more. Is there a jinx? Why does such a black cloud seem to hang over this organization? Only time will tell.

The internet provides a funny piece called "the curse of Bobby Layne". The site talks about the 1958 trading card for Layne. When Layne was traded to the Steelers, his trading card had him in a Lions blue jersey. Was the mistake because he was traded so quickly, or was this an omen of things to come?

The site goes on to say "if someone or something is truly cursed, no matter what they did, no matter how hard they try, something always keeps them from succeeding. Sometimes this bending of fate leaves behind an almost humorous bi-product that lingers long after the event". The site describes several Lion humiliations since Layne was traded from the Lions. In 1966, coach Harry Gilmer was pummeled by snowballs from Lion fans in Tiger Stadium. Fans started chanting "bye bye Harry". The Lions lost that game 28-16 and Mr. Ford fired Gilmore after the 4-9-1 record that year. He was replaced by Joe Schmidt. A fan uprising against the Lions – could it happen again?

In 1962, the Lions drafted John Hadl. They tried to convince him to switch positions and play running back. He was a quarterback in college. He thought the Lions were crazy, refused to sign with them, and ended up on the San Diego Chargers. He went on to become a six time pro bowler. Why can't the Lions recognize talent when it's right in front of them?

Another humiliation involved draft day. "Is it possible to trade your number one pick and not know it? In 1974, the Lions forgot that they traded their first round pick which was #13 to New Orleans with a player. The Lions attempted to make the 13th pick, and were reminded that they had traded it.

In 1987 Wayne Fontes was arrested and eventually arraigned on cocaine possession and two drunken driving charges. He pleads not guilty and eventually is promoted to Head Coach. After everything Mr. Ford did for Fontes, Wayne thanks him by suing the Lions in 1999 claiming his back was injured while working for the Lions and he could no longer work as a coach in the NFL. This might have been because he wasn't a very good coach! He lost the suit.

❖❖❖

During the early 70's the Minnesota Vikings tortured us more than any other team. They had won 13 straight over the Lions until Oct. 20th 1974 when the Lions finally ended the streak with a 20-16 win. Before that, Al and I had multiple "I don't believe it" experiences followed by two or three days of depression all caused by our arch rival Vikings. Sept. 20, 1971; Errol Mann misses a 33 yard field goal to tie the game as time expired. Dec.11th 1971; the Lions lose to the Vikings turning the ball over six times. The Vikings scored a touchdown in this game after the Lions blocked a field goal and the Vikings recovered the ball in the end zone for a touchdown. Even when they made a great play, it went the Vikings way. Nov. 12th 1972; Bobby Bryant blocks a 33 yard field goal attempt that would have won the game for the Lions as time ran out. On Nov.7th 1973, we had another Viking victory that included a blocked punt for a touchdown.

The "purple people eaters" and Fran Tarkington tortured us for years. How fitting it was in the December 2004 game that the Lions blow an extra point to force overtime against none other than the Minnesota Vikings. It brought back quite a few memories - all bad.

A few more horror stories from the early 70's. On Dec.26th, 1970 Detroit lost 5-0 in the playoffs to the Dallas Cowboys. Greg Landry was one of the best quarter backs of the past 40 years, and we had our all pro corner Lem Barney on the team. Recently I heard Lem Barney in a radio interview say that that game bothered him so much, that to this day some 34 years later, he did not even want to talk about it. Sept. 29th 1974 the Lions lost a 21-19 decision to the Green Bay Packers. Again, the Lions have a punt blocked for a safety.

❖❖❖

In 49 years since their last championship, the Lions have had 29 losing seasons, 16 winning and 4 .500 seasons. Their all time record is 483-539-32. We have had one playoff victory since 1957. It seems almost impossible for one of the original franchises in the NFL.

I want to describe some of the happy times I have had being a Lions fan. Fans loved Charlie Sanders. When Al and I were teenagers, we would throw a football across his bed and one of us would try to catch it stretched out horizontally the way Sanders did. He was the greatest Lions receiver I have ever seen. I would say Herman Moore was the second best. Charlie Sanders had one of his great days November 26th, 1970, against the Oakland Raiders. I recall the

Lions being down 14-0 at half time and winning 28-14. Sanders made two of his classic touchdown catches; I was watching close-by near that end zone, and remembered what incredible catches those were. Tiger Stadium was very loud that day.

Detroit Lions football fans are amazing; they never give up. The crowds at the Silver dome were so loud, there was no question it was intimidating to visiting teams. A majority of games have been sold out at home; even at the Silver Dome with 80,000 capacity, I bet 80% of games were sold out or near sell outs. The support for this team has been outstanding, especially considering how poorly they have performed with few results since 1957.

Our favorite Lion players since 1970 in order of athletic ability and fan appeal; Barry Sanders, Lem Barney, Charlie Sanders, Billie Sims, Herman Moore, Joe Schmitt, Alex Karris, Al Bubba Baker, Robert Porcher, Eddie Murray, Jason Hanson, Greg Landry, Gary Danielson, Shawn Rogers, Mel Grey and Chris Spielman.

Barry Sanders was simply unbelievable. The greatest football player by far I have ever seen as a Lion. He was the main reason to look forward to watching the Lions for 10 years. I remember the day he retired. My buddies and I were on a five day golfing trip in Northern Michigan. We were at dinner one night after golfing 36 holes that day. My friend said, "I just heard that Barry Sanders announced his retirement". My friend is a practical joker, so I thought he was up to his old tricks. I bet him $20 that it was a ploy; when he thanked me for the $20, and put it in his pocket, I realized that the Lions worst nightmare had been realized. How could Barry do it? Everyone was so looking forward to him becoming the all time rushing leader in the next year. Lions football has never been the same since that day. A player of his caliber comes along maybe every 50 years. To this day, I will be glad to debate anyone that Barry Sanders was the greatest running back who has ever played the game.

One of my great thrills associated with the Lions was having the opportunity to meet Barry Sanders a few years after he retired. I was at a golf dome during a nasty winter night in the Detroit area. There was hardly anyone there when I came to the putting green after hitting balls. I look up and see Barry Sanders as the only other person on the green with me. I recognized him immediately, and had to meet him. He was so polite and friendly. I couldn't believe it. He talked to me with no ego or star power. We mostly talked about golf; he loved the game. He met my son and daughter and gave them his autograph. I told him I met Lawrence Taylor at a golf tournament and couldn't believe how big he was. I said to Barry, "how could you survive a hit from a guy that big"? He answered, "now you know why I ran so fast!" Barry said Lawrence got him a few times, and it didn't feel very good. I offered to take Barry golfing at U of M someday since he had not played that course and wanted to; I gave him my phone number and told him I would be honored to golf with him. He thanked me and said "he just might take me up on it". He never called, but what a gentleman he was to me and my children; I will never forget meeting him that day.

Chapter 4

On being a Lion's fan - long term mental health concerns
A. Sports in the USA - an insatiable need for entertainment

Through the years, the amount of confusion, bad coaching, and a general lack of confidence has destroyed many Lions teams. Making mistakes at the most crucial points of a game is a Lions trademark. These are the things that bad teams do on a regular basis and why the fans have suffered through so many seasons.

Our coach to start the 1976 season was Rick Forzano, who was fired after a 1-3 start (APPENDIX A). He coached for two plus seasons and had 15 wins and 17 losses (did you ever notice how much he would pat the Lions players on their butts?). Tommy Hudspeth replaced him and went five wins, five loses the rest of the 1976 season. He coached through the 1977 season when he was 6-8. Monte Clark took over from 1978-1984. Clark's seven years as Coach was the second longest stint in Lions' history behind eight years for George Wilson (1957-1964), and eight years for Wayne Fontes (1989-1996). Who would have guessed that Fontes would be the most successful coach since 1957. He ended with 66 wins and 67 losses! He was our most successful coach in 49 years. This says it all.

Why can't the Lions ever seem to get a great coach? Other teams seem to be able to. Bill Belichick, Bill Parcells, Mike Shanahan, Bill Walsh, Joe Gibbs, Marv Levy, Mike Ditka, John Madden, Don Shula, Chuck Noll, Tom Landry, Bud Grant and Vince Lombardi. All won Super Bowls or got their team there more than once. What makes a coach great in the NFL? Hard to answer; you obviously need great players, but leadership and schemes are key.

◆◆◆

NFL football is filled with injuries for all teams; thus the reason it is necessary to have a 53 player roster. But it seems to us that the Lions have way more injuries than most teams. In 1982 to have 10 key players injured and then have Sims break his hand - what are the odds (APPENDIX B)? These players were obviously injured in the pre-season or in training camp. In 2003, the injury to Charles Rogers during practice hurt the team significantly (APPENDIX F). His broken collar bone was re-injured in the first game this year and has cost him almost his entire first two seasons.

The Lions lost games in the last minutes of games an incredible number of times. This is what tortures fans so much; they often seem so close to being good. Maybe the Vikings announcer was right Dec. 19, 2004 when he said "the Lions just don't think they can win."

I realize as the games are summarized from the past how often bad things happened around my birthday Oct. 26th. Chuck Hughes death, Billy Sims career cut short. Let's see what other memories the Lions have provided for my birthday week.

The Lions have always struggled with their red zone execution. Inside your opponents 20 yard line is where the game is won or lost offensively. The great teams score a lot of touchdowns from this position. The bad teams always seem to come close, but often have to settle for field goals. The NFL is a league that requires touchdowns to win. I would love to see the statistics on team field goals over the past 30 years. I am guessing the Lions have more than most teams. That is why we have had such successful kickers over the years; Errol Mann, Eddie Murray and Jason Hanson. They had a lot of opportunities to kick field goals after drives would stall.

❖❖❖

Let's look at the quarterbacks since 1965. Greg Landry was one of our best. I remember Bill Munson, Carl Sweetan, Milt Plum, Eric Hipple, Gary Danielson (one of our best), Chuck Long, Rodney Peete, Andre Ware, Eric Kramer (he won a playoff game – this makes him special!), Scott Mitchell, Charlie Batch, Joey Harrington. I hope I'm not forgetting anyone. What happened to the days of Bobby Layne? I was in diapers when he was winning championships for Detroit. The only great Lion quarterback, and I miss it!

Why have the Lions struggled to get a great quarterback? Or, were these quarterbacks good, but were in a bad system, with bad coaching? None of them went on to greatness with other teams. Most of them never got a starting position again. Some never played in the NFL again. I guess our college scouting staff has never been very good. One could wonder what a great quarterback would do as a Lion? Let's dream for a moment and say the Lions had Payton Manning as their QB next year. How about Tom Brady, Dante Culpepper, Donavan McNabb, or Michael Vick? Is it the coach that makes the quarterback, or the quarterback that makes the coach? Or is it the offensive scheme, personnel and leadership that are the keys? If we had one of these top QB's, it is possible the Lions would win 10 games next year? Why can't we seem to draft the right quarterbacks?

I often wonder about players careers being determined in part by which team drafts them. What if Barry Sanders would have been drafted first that year by the Packers, instead of second by the Lions? Barry would have had several Super Bowl rings playing with Brett Farve. Could you imagine those two together? What if the Lions took Randy Moss instead of Terry Fair? What if they would have understood the potential of a young man playing football 30 miles from Detroit at the University of Michigan a few years ago? Why did New England take Tom Brady in the sixth round? They must have seen something in him. It's probably good for Brady that Detroit did not take him; who knows where his career would be today. I met Tom Brady when he was a 19 year old at U of M. He was working behind the counter at the U of M golf course and recognized his name tag, as the back up QB at Michigan. I remember how young he looked. A very nice young man, I shook his hand and wished him luck in football – he did pretty well, what do you think?

❖❖❖

The Lions just never seemed to win close games. Their effort has always been solid, but there is no replacement for playmakers and great coaching. We have had very few game breaking type of players since 1957. The main ones have been Barry Sanders, Herman Moore, Charlie Sanders, Lem Barney, Mel Grey and Eddie Drummond, Al Baker, and Billie Sims. We have never had a quarterback that just willed us to victory. We have never had a coach that out smarted the other coach. I would argue that the Lions have had some very good talent over these years, but have had terrible head coaching. This is the reason they have lost so many games after leading at halftime. This is why they never seem to win the game in the fourth quarter of a close one. It seems it is a combination of poor strategy and a lack of leadership instilling confidence and calm in the players' at the most crucial times, which has led to failure.

Lions fans get so frustrated over games like the one against the Packers on Oct. 25, 1987 (APPENDIX C). Green Bay jumps to a 24-0 lead, but the Lions fight back to take the lead 33-31 late in the game. The Packers kick a 45 yard field goal to go up 34-33, but the Lions keep fighting and drive the ball down in field goal position with a shot at winning the game. A 45 yard field goal attempt misses as time runs out. I'm guessing it was missed by Eddie Murray. Although we have had solid kickers over these torturous years, we have missed most big field goals to win games. Detroit has not been able to perform when it counts the most! Can you imagine how frustrating this game was for the players that killed themselves to come back, and never gave up losing the game that way? Same story over 49 years; the offense takes the lead, the defense can't hold, and a missed field goal to lose. It has happened many, many times.

◆◆◆

As these games were reviewed, one that really stood out for me was the Sept. 6, 1992 loss to the Bears 27-24 on opening day. The day before, I broke my kneecap falling down a hill on a golf course (very athletic, I know). My orthopedic surgeon operated on me Sunday morning to put the bone back together with wire and two pins. It was very nice of Dr. Zeminik to come to work on a Sunday. I told him and the anesthesiologist that it was opening day for the Lions, and when given the choice of general or spinal for the operation, I chose the spinal. It was opening day for the Lions, a new season - new hope. I didn't want to be sleeping after the surgery and miss the game. I also asked them if they could finish and get me back to the room by kickoff. I have always been a passionate Lions fan; does this prove it? I remember the Lions losing the game on the last play with one second to go. I was having a great day!

Why are football fans so passionate? Why do Lions fans never give up the dream? Sport is one of the mainstays of "male bonding" in America. We go to the games with buddies, watch them together, and talk about them on the phone when life is too hectic to get together. Men don't talk about emotions, family, job satisfaction or most other life matters. But when a team wins a professional or college championship, why do fans feel so much a part of it? It's the players that have killed themselves, preparing for years to experience that moment. It is their team, not ours. We must feel that they represent us, our city, or our Universities - it speaks to the pride people have in the area they live in. For some people, it makes them feel special. They feel that they are part of something really big, and in their own small way feel they were part of the championship, because they screamed and rooted their team on to victory. Some people have very low self esteem and are not happy in their lives. For those few days or weeks, they are lifted to a different level and enjoy the adrenaline rush that can accompany a sport title. When the rush is over though, it's back to dealing with their lives and reality.

One of the major reasons football is the most popular sport in the United States is that there is only one game played per week. Each game holds far greater importance than in the other major sports. It is the ultimate team game – breakdowns in any area can prevent winning. What gives a team the ability to win the big one? To win a game that clinches a playoff spot, or one that sends you to the Super Bowl? I believe it is the head coach. They form the strategy for the game, play calling, motivation and adjustments at halftime. Even Wayne Fontes who took the Lions further than any other coach since 1957, had a terrible playoff record.

Sports as a hobby helped me through my teenage and young adult years more than anything aside from my family. It provided a sense of passion in my life (while I was discovering women). It provided a healthy escape from stress. It teaches young people so many important values. It teaches you that life is competitive in the world of work and career. Sport teaches one the importance of a team – the need to do your job with the greatest effort so others will also be successful. It teaches individual responsibility. It teaches kids to be good sports; not to rub it in when you win – and how to accept losing without giving up the next game. It teaches people to realize how far they can push themselves; accomplishing things one never thought they could. It gives one a sense of self esteem and the joy you feel when you have had a great performance. Sports are an integral part of American culture.

It will be hard to forget the days after 9/11 when it was important to begin the healing process. President Bush walked on the field in Yankee Stadium to throw out the first pitch. He was wearing a bullet proof vest, and the secret service did not want him to do this. He showed courage and leadership that day. Sport brings people together working for a common cause. We needed sports on that day. Few things can produce that kind of passion and emotion.

Years ago my buddy Al heard a call to a radio show. The caller was very depressed and told the host he was going to kill himself at 6 p.m. on Saturday. When the host asked why 6 p.m. Saturday, the guy said, "Because he wanted to watch the Tigers Saturday afternoon." Sports do give people something to look forward to, even in the worst of circumstances.

The Tigers won two championships in 1968 and 1984; the Red Wings won three from 1997-2002; the Pistons won three in 1988, 1989 and 2003. The University of Michigan won both basketball and football championships. Michigan State won two basketball championships. I was two years old when the Lions won their last championship in 1957. I don't remember it! Our Red Wings finally broke through winning the Stanley Cup in 1997 after 42 years without a championship. They had one of the best coaches in the history of sports in Scotty Bowman. The Lions have never had great coaches or quarterbacks, which are the two most important positions on an NFL team. I was too young to remember the one great quarterback we had, Bobby Layne. Buddy Parker was the coach from 1951-1956 and was part of our three championships. I would love to know why he resigned as coach August 12, 1957. He must have been considered our greatest coach. The game has clearly gotten more complicated since 1957. I think our best quarterbacks were Landry and Danielson. What would our team have been like if we ever had a Brett Favre, Payton Manning, Dan Marino or Joe Montana?

◆◆◆

Am I being too hard on the Lions? They are not the only professional sports organization that has been bad over 50 years. The Cubs in baseball, the L.A. Clippers and Cleveland Cavaliers in basketball, the Cardinals, Saints and Browns in football have had similar histories. It's the nature of sports that some franchises never seem to be able to put a winner together. The hope of improvement, the entertainment of the games, the occasional great player who is worshipped all serve the fan. And the dream that maybe one day we will play for a championship.

The term fan comes from the word fanatics. Clearly, too many people go overboard in their desire and emotional need for their team to win. You see it in fan behavior, when too much drinking takes place, and swearing and vulgarity are heard by kids. Why do so many people, particularly men, put so much into their teams? I believe it represents what is missing in a person's life emotionally. People look for things in their lives to fill in missing holes. Troubled families, bad marriages, drinking or drug addictions and disappointing careers all create a sense of emptiness. Others go about adult life with no passion. They are emotionally dead. Life has become too boring, too stressful or both.

Other fans use sports as a healthy outlet and pause from adult routines. There is a magic about getting lost in a game. Time does not exist, problems are temporarily gone. The players and the teams are representing you and the city you live in. There is a deep sense of pride that people have in their teams.

How does a team like the Dallas Cowboys make it to eight Super Bowls? They have the most appearances of any team. What about teams like San Francisco, Denver, Green Bay, Pittsburgh, Oakland, Miami and New England make them so successful? Do they know something the Lion's don't? Are their owners wiser about football matters; have they hired better presidents or GM's? How do they recognize talent in coaches and players? I was recently reading a national football magazine with the cover reading "the NFL's greatest 100 players." Were there any Lions? Nope. There was one honorable mention in Shawn Rogers. Could that explain the terrible record the last several years?

❖ ❖ ❖

Being a Lions fan can be hazardous to your health. What happens to a fan when they have endured so much pain and suffering year after year? Depression sets in first. You find yourself a little down and discouraged most Sundays around 4 p.m. I guess I'll get to those chores I've been putting off all weekend. As a kid it meant ending the weekend on a downer – back to school tomorrow. As an adult, it's back to the work jungle on Monday morning. Listening to post game shows and reading the sports section Monday for the post mortem is a tradition. The radio announcer Mark Champion tries his best to be objective, but he has suffered as much as we have. You can tell that he is also a great fan of the Lions. The reflection in his voice after a particularly painful loss is obvious. There have been times I was worried that he might jump out of the booth! "Botched snap; game over."

After years of Sunday evening depression, a Lions fan may find himself not caring anymore, maybe not watching the whole game – just checking the score now and then. It is here that emotional distance and pulling away from the team takes place. "Who cares anyway, it's only a sport, I have more important things in my life to worry about. I'm not wasting my energy on them!" A fan with season tickets may begin thinking about not renewing them next year. You may start hoping that fans stay away in protest, so the team makes less money and begins to show ownership that we mean business. This is when the most toxic emotion begins to creep in – anger. Fans will take an incredible amount of poor performances and years of mediocrity. Why? It is because of their intense need to escape the pressures of adult life. It's still one of the healthier ways to escape for a period of time.

As anger begins to set in sometimes after year forty, the fan realizes that this is now serious. You begin ranting to your buddies about the Lions. "Can you believe how they lost Sunday?" You begin to say things like "we could coach the team to 16 wins in four years." Wouldn't that be a great reality show! My buddy, who had been a successful high school football coach and I take over the team for a year – we keep the offensive and defensive coordinators. How many games would the Lions win? Would we go 0-16? I have told friends that I thought we could win 4-6 games; am I nuts? I know people in Detroit would watch this reality show. George Plimpton would be proud!

Along with the anger vowing to stop being a fan forever, delusions may begin to set in as the one described previously. "We could coach the team to four wins." I'm following through with my threat to not buy my season tickets next year. My friends' brother may want them – should I keep them in my name? What if they get good in the next few years? Am I being a disloyal fan? Am I just a front runner? Maybe 50 years is too little to give the team I love. I should be tougher and endure the pain until I'm 80 years old – it's only another 30 years!

Should the Lions begin putting the following warning on the back of their tickets? Caution! Being a Lion's fan for any prolonged period (20 years plus) may lead to the following symptoms: depression, anger, rage, nausea, vomiting, delusions, and suicide. Check with your physician before committing to this team.

◆◆◆

Can you imagine what it feels like to own a professional sports team? What it must feel like to be Mr. Ford or his son. How badly they want to win a championship! What a great hobby to have, trying to put a football team together that becomes the best. I know it's a business, and the Lions have probably made a fair amount of money over the years. When a person owns Ford Motor Company, they are probably doing pretty well financially. How much money does one man or family need? So when I said it's an amazing hobby for the Fords, I think I'm right. The pride of winning a championship has got to mean more to the Fords than the money. Does Mr. Ford feel like a failure? Certainly not in business, I'm sure. It has to get to him that he has tried everything he knows to give the city and the fans a winning team.

Our country is entertainment starved! We crave distractions from life constantly. I believe this is why people follow sports with such a passion. Too many people hate their work, are not happy in their relationships and look for an escape from the stressful adult world in many ways. Some are healthier than others. When you watch your team on Sunday, you lose yourself completely. Your worries are gone, your problems can wait. Passion is the other key to following sports. People must have passion in their lives. Something that gets them excited, interested, motivated. Without passion, life can seem without meaning. People find their passions through careers, hobbies, relationships, family, money, sex, movies, theatre, music, computers and sports. Hollywood and sports represent huge entertainment, distraction, and money. Actors and athletes make unbelievable money. $20 million per movie; Michael Vick a 100 million dollar contract, NBA players making 17 million per year; baseball players getting a 10 year 250 million dollar contract. Capitalism is a beautiful thing! I always wished I could get 50,000 people to pay $30 per ticket to watch me do a therapy session with a troubled client. Not exciting enough? I have several friends who are physicians and make a good living, but not enough when they save a persons life! My old liberal beliefs are coming out, I apologize. Our priorities are a bit backwards in America, but it's the best we've got.

◆◆◆

I've been reading Charlie Sanders new book, "Tales from the Detroit Lions." When he played in 1962, he was making $16,000/yr. What has happened to the salaries, revenue and business of sports is amazing. Do you think that the athletes like Charlie Sanders resent the money these young men are making today? It seems that the multi-year contracts create some athletes who just coast. There is little incentive to get better. Although the level of talent is unbelievable today (training, weight lifting, nutrition…) it seems we have a lot of "spoiled brats" who don't appreciate what they have. The distance and anger between fans and players that has occurred over the past 20 years is very predictable. When the average fan is making $40,000/yr at their job and the average athlete is making one to two million per year, it has to effect how fans view athletes.

Terrell Owens was a perfect example of this. He is a spoiled brat who was always used to getting his way; throwing a tantrum because he felt he was under paid by the Eagles. His contract was for 42 million dollars over seven years! So what does he do? He throws a fit and decides to be a bad boy, causing disruption of the team, causing chaos, and getting himself fired. The Eagles did the right thing.

We see some problems that have arisen from this insatiable need for stimulation and entertainment. There are so many choices today that one has regarding how they spend their free time. The internet, cable, video games, sports, movies, vacations and hobbies are all available. We are on an adrenaline overload! You see it with young kids and teenagers. Most are able to mature and be guided in the direction of maturity and responsibility in preparation for the adult world. Too many however, get stuck in the entertainment, hedonistic world of play and avoidance of developmental growth. My 18 year old son is an example. His whole life is about entertainment. I was never a great disciplinarian, so some of the fault lies with his mother and I. But teens today have so much to choose from it is amazing.

I believe that some of the passion has gone out of professional sports due to the amazing salaries. The average fan doesn't connect to the athlete or the team, because they just can't relate to their world. There is also a sense that athletes from earlier days were more loyal and dedicated to the cities and sport than modern day athletes. It seems that greed and money dominate. I believe some of this resentment towards professional athletes and entertainers was responsible for the recent NBA brawl here in Detroit earlier this year. For these reasons, many people are turning to high school and college sports, to re-capture the purity of sport. Young people playing for the thrill of competition and victory; representing their high school, college or recreational team.

The recent NHL lock out is another example of problems in professional sports, and how much of it has become strictly business. As a fan of hockey, I have been disgusted with the greed on both sides. Fighting about a salary cap; will it be $42 million or $49 Million? The answer, if the season will be saved, is coming in the next few days in February of 2005. My anger and that of many fans is that it comes down to an average NHL player saying "I want my cap to allow me to make 1.4 million instead of 1 million". Owners have the risk of running a business, so I tend to support their side more for this reason. In this case, I feel both sides are wrong. The owners can clearly hold out longer because they can sustain the losses more than the players. The players are starting to miss their pay checks. The average fan most likely earns $30,000 – $150,000 and have a hard time feeling bad for players fighting for an extra half million dollars! We all have bosses or owners to deal with. I am a social worker in the public schools and make $84,000 per year with a Masters degree. Even though teachers get significant vacation time (so do pro athletes!), their jobs are rather difficult. I believe that people resent the amount of money professional athletes make today, especially when you see some with bad attitudes.

❖❖❖

When it counts the most! Let's look at two playoff games. The 1991 NFC championship game we lost to Washington and the 1993 playoff lose to the Packers. We had a great team that year in 1991; we were 12-4 and had just won the only playoff game since 1957. The reason to discuss this game has to do with the score at halftime. It was Washington 17-10. 30 minutes of football left to go to get to the Super Bowl, and the Lions are down one touchdown. How does the team completely collapse, and lose the second half 24-0! It's coaching. Clearly the Redskins were a great team, as they went on to win the Super Bowl, but they had a guy on the other sidelines named Joe Gibbs. We had Wayne Fontes.

My brother met Wayne Fontes at a bar one night near the Silver dome. He was very friendly and talked with my brother for over an hour about the Lions. He remembers Fontes telling him that the problem with the team is that the offense scored too quickly. My brother thought that was a little strange. He was obviously talking about a ball control offense which eats up the clock and keeps guys like Brett Favre off the field. But, if you can score too quickly, you should be able to beat teams 49-21 every game. After Fontes left the bar, my brother talked to a personnel guy from the Lions, quite high up in administration. He told my brother that they kept getting Fontes all these solid players, but that he was an "idiot" and didn't know how to use them. He did not care for Fontes, who of course we now know had the best results of any coach for the Lions since 1957. I wonder if he was such a good coach, or perhaps the results might have had to do more with a guy named Sanders!

The 1993 playoff loss to the Packers 28-24 on a last minute 40 yard TD pass from Favre to Sharpe is another great example of complete and utter futility. We all remember Sharpe being wide open for the touchdown catch, not a Lion player within 20 yards of him. When it counts the most! What a great time for a miscommunication and a blown defensive coverage.

❖❖❖

Reviewing these past five seasons, I realize that passionate Lions fans have had only two exciting moments in the past 49 years. The first was the playoff win over Dallas in 1991. The second was watching Barry Sanders run throughout his career. This man was unbelievable, and I still feel bad for Barry that he was not drafted first by the Green Bay Packers the year he came out. He would have been wearing several Super Bowl rings to show the champion that he was!

Barry ran for two touchdowns on Oct.12, 1997 against Tampa Bay of 80 yards plus; the only time this has ever been done in the NFL(APPENDIX E). That year, he added another 80 plus yard touch down run; three in one year – how amazing is that? In 1998, Barry ran for 150 yards plus in a game for the 25th time in his career, another all time NFL record. He also had 15 runs of over 50 yards at that point in 1998; another all time record. When Sanders retired, my heart went out of the Lions – I'm not sure I will ever get it back.

Chapter 5

The year I finally snapped; was I really rooting against the Lions? A. The 2004 season and aftermath - I can't watch this anymore!

The season just finished a week ago in December, 2004, so the web sight does not have the game summaries yet. Let's see what sticks out from this 2004 season. We start strong, breaking the 24 game road losing streak in Chicago. Unfortunately, Charles Rogers' collar bone is also broken. There were two other great road wins at Atlanta and the Giants. The 4-2 start got everyone excited. I was at the Washington game which we lost to go to 4-4; a bad snap led to a blocked punt and TD which was big. A crucial home game for Detroit; and the game I consider changed the season for Detroit. A win, and we would have been 5-3 the first half. It was also the most boring NFL game I have ever attended. A friend of mine from Pittsburgh agreed that it was the worst game he had ever seen. Other highlights include blowing leads at Minnesota of 19-7 and at Green Bay of 13-0. The missed extra point at home against the Vikings, which would have forced overtime was classic. And then, to end the year right, the refs give the game to Detroit at home against the Bears, on the worst call I have ever seen in the NFL. They can't even lose right! Now the Lions get the tenth pick in the draft instead of the fourth. We can't forget Jacksonville; when Eddie Drummond runs his second punt return back for a TD forcing over time, and hardly anyone rushes Eddie to congratulate him – that's a good sign.

These past four years have been so painful for Lion fans, it is hard to describe. Sixteen wins in four years; what more can you say. The game of Nov. 9, 2003 was amazing. The Lions beat the Bears 12-10 while rushing for only 12 yards! Isn't that some kind of record? And to make it worse, the leading rusher was our receiver Eddie Swinton, who ran for nine yards on an end around. How can an NFL team run for 12 yards in a game? It is hard to believe they actually won this game.

Where do we go from here? I've decided to keep my two season tickets for one more year, so I can have a chance at a ticket for Super Bowl 40. My mental illness must be creeping in; before I said I was done with the team, and canceling my season tickets. I have to find a good therapist; I happen to know several and will be glad to refer any distraught Lions fan that requires professional help. It is very understanding – a person actually has to be very strong to cope with the Lions since 1957.

Steve Mariucci said "enough anguish," at his final press conference. I think he understands what this city has gone through with its football team over the years. Is he the guy to change things? Can he turn things around and get us to the Super Bowl? Although his coaching the first two years has been disappointing, he certainly comes across as a very bright, likable person. We are all pulling for you Mooch!

It's January 8, 2005 – the NFL playoffs, how exciting! But where are the Lions? Oh, they didn't make the playoffs; there is always next year, right? I see ex-Lion players on other teams. Rueben Droughns from Denver, who rushed for over 1200 yards this year; maybe the system helped him succeed. James Mungro of the Colts; he seems to be doing well – it might help to have your quarterback be Payton Manning! Hey, there's Tom Moore, the offensive coordinator of the

Colts top offense in the league. Didn't he used to work for the Lions? There are many stories like this. The most amazing is when Don Shula was an assistant coach on the Lions. Didn't he end up having a good career?

The announcers are saying that it has been a long time since Denver has won a playoff game; all the way back to 1998 when they won their back to back Super Bowls. Don't we feel sorry for them?

It's the week of January 24, 2005. It will be the Eagles and the Patriots in the 39th Super Bowl in Jacksonville. I don't see how the Eagles can win this game, but you never know. Tom Brady will attempt to run his record to 9-0 in the playoffs; absolutely incredible. Of course, the Lions talk continues. Should the Lions trade Williams or Rogers and a draft pick for Randy Moss? Detroit has hired its new offensive coordinator; a 64 year old friend of Steve Mariucci from the 49'ers. The 49'ers had one of the worst offenses in the league the last few years, and last year was 2-14; the worst record in the NFL. It seems the league is a "good old boys network." Tresman was available and very well thought of, but he clearly wasn't smart enough for the Lions. It seems that Mariucci has brought in a coach that will be an aide to him – obviously Mariucci wants to call the offense himself. This coach will probably retire in a few years; why don't the Lions ever seem to hire the right people? If the next two seasons don't show significant improvement, Millen, Mariucci and Harrington will probably all be gone.

❖❖❖

I have settled down after the season ended three weeks ago in January 2005. I don't hate the Lions anymore. I do believe they have a legitimate chance of winning 9 or 10 games next year. It's not my delusions talking either, is it? Part of the illness has to do with going through a recovery period a month after the season is over, and then having the delusions return. I need to see my shrink soon; I am getting healthy – I am recognizing the symptoms of relapse. By July, all of the horrible memories of the last 48 years will have faded. Fans will be ready to predict a playoff season for our beloved Lions. The hope of a new season is always exciting; the problem has always been when they have to play the games. It's like a death and a re-birth. Fans never stop hoping, no matter how realistic it is or isn't.

Today's sports talk radio subject, in February 2005, from Tony Ortiz is which will demand more attention on Sept. 11, 2005; the Tigers in a pennant race, or the opening game of the NFL season for the Lions? As much as Detroit would love a successful baseball season, there is no question that Tony Ortiz is correct when he says that the NFL rules in Detroit. This is a city that is obsessed with its football team, much like the Eagle fans who lost the Super Bowl two days ago, in February of 2005. The ex-governor of Philadelphia recently said that if the Eagles were to lose the NFL championship game two weeks ago for the fourth consecutive year, there would be no one going to work on Monday, because the streets would be filled with the dead bodies of Eagle fans who had jumped! Detroit has a similar passion. I can't imagine what this town would be like if we ever made it to the big game. We talk about the Lions 365 days a year. NFL football is by far the dominant sport in this country. The Pistons might be the next most talked about because of their recent championship.

The Lions signed two players yesterday, March 7, 2005. Its official, we're going to the Super Bowl! These are the two players that will put us over the top; the players we have been waiting 47 years for since our last championship. Seriously, they were two solid signings that should improve the team. They signed a hard hitting safety and a reliable tight end. It will also allow the team more flexibility with their first round pick at number 10 to take a player other than a safety. The sport talk shows are buzzing! The safety, Kennedy, reportedly was at the airport about to go interview with the Miami Dolphins when the Lions closed the deal; I hope he doesn't regret not getting on that plane; maybe not today, but…. does he understand the history of our Lions?

❖❖❖

Is it possible my Lions induced delusions are coming back? I'm actually starting to feel some hope for next season. The players they signed this week in March of 2005, along with an expected signing of a solid back-up quarterback has got me thinking 10 wins and a playoff appearance. We are also getting Charles Roger back, hopefully Boss Bailey and the 10th pick in the draft. The anger over last season is starting to go away. This is the life of a Detroit Lions fan; sometime within a month or two of the Super Bowl, we begin to have hope. This is because we are six months away from opening day and have no chance of losing yet.

I probably should make an appointment with a therapist, since these delusions of success with the Lions can return quickly. I must return to the reality of the past 48 years, shouldn't I? It is a lot of fun to fantasize and pretend that we will win though. What's wrong with living in a fantasy world? Don't adults need to escape the real world?

There is big news about Mark Champion losing his spot as the Lions announcer. I have a lot of mixed feelings. He is a great announcer with a tremendous voice. You can tell that he loves the Lions as he was calling the games; when the Lions lost a "heartbreaker," as they often did, you could hear the pain in his voice. He reflected what tortured Lions' fans were feeling. I have told friends that I was worried that Champion would jump out of the booth after some particularly hard losses. He became more critical of the team in recent years with good reason. His honesty was warranted. He has been the voice of the Lions for 16 years and Lions football won't be the same without him. If the Lions ever have any success, it won't feel right without Mark Champion. Talk about someone who has suffered through the tough times with this team. Maybe he will get the play by play of another NFL team and he will get to see what real football looks like! He is the radio announcer for our world champion Detroit Pistons, so someone can still recognize his talents.

Mike McMahon signed a two year deal with the Eagles. Good for him; I met him twice, a very nice guy. I was always upset last year when Harrington was playing poorly, and they thought so little of McMahon, that they did not play him. I felt there is no reason to sign a back-up who is only going to play if there is an injury. A third string quarter back can do that. Now we wait to see if the Lions sign Brad Johnson or Jeff Garcia as the back-up who will compete for the starting job with Harrington. Both of these quarterbacks are at the end of their careers. If they were really good still, do you think their teams would have let them go? The 48 year problem of poor quarterbacking for the Lions continues, with no end in sight.

The Lions signed Jeff Garcia to a one year contract to back up/ compete with Joey Harrington for the QB position. Garcia has had two poor years and is 35 years old; he was in the pro bowl three years while in San Francisco playing for Mariucci. His receivers those years were Jerry Rice and Terrell Owens – I think that might have something to do with his success. Anyway, it was considered a good signing. Someone should let Garcia know his career is over and he will be going out without a Super Bowl ring. Does he know anything about the last 48 years in Detroit? The next big date for Lion junkies is at the end of April when we take the 10th pick in the draft and try to find that "Tom Brady" quarterback late in the rounds that we can develop when it's obvious that Joey is a bust.

Dre' Bly was quoted in the paper today, March 22, 2005, as saying that it is time for the players to step up and win this year. No more excuses blaming the organization or the coaches. He said he came to Detroit because he believed in Steve Mariucci, and this is the year to win, especially with the Super Bowl in Detroit. Does that mean he thinks the Lions should make it to the Super Bowl this year? Very inspiring, don't you agree?

The sports talk show discussed a report that the Lions will be meeting with the quarterback out of Utah this week because there is a chance he may be available at the 10th pick in the draft. Most likely, he will be taken before, but just in case. The discussion centered around the question of why the Lions would consider drafting a quarterback; especially with the first pick. There was a sense that if they took this guy, they might decide to cut Joey Harrington because they want to avoid a large bonus that is do to him by June. Garcia would then be the starter while they develop the college kid. It's April and we are talking football! As the host of the show said, "any time there is news about the Lions, it becomes the first thing you need to talk about."

It turns out that the Lions management basically lied to the media about the Utah quarterback. They said that a tight end out of Stanford with the same first and last name (Alex Smith) was in for an evaluation. After a week or so, the media found out that both players were in for an interview; the tight end and the quarterback. Why would the Lions lie to the media? People believe that the Lions were trying to protect Harrington's "fragile ego." I don't understand how this organization does business – based on their record since 1957, obviously not very effectively.

It is nine days before the 2005 NFL draft on April 14, 2005. The sports radio shows are talking Lions today, after their schedule was released for this year. The disturbed, delusional fans were calling in with predictions of 10, 11 and even a 12 win season. This disease can creep up on a person very quickly, without warning. It is sad that so many fine Detroit people suffer from this incurable illness. I must discover a cure for this problem.

Draft day is two days away. The Lions may take a very fast, physical linebacker out of Texas. There has been a lot of talk about taking a quarterback from Florida State, McPherson in the third round. He had some problems that involved jail time, but as long as he can throw a ball and win games…. This is a very exciting time for Lions fans; a time when hope is at it's highest. I have to admit, that even I believe this should be a good year for the Lions. Will this change when they actually have to play the games in September?

❖❖❖

The draft was Saturday. It was our Super Bowl. If you heard the callers on the sports radio shows, you would hear the excitement that only a draft day can bring a Lion's fan. This is as good as it gets. We pick Mike Williams out of USC – a huge, fast wide receiver. I have to admit that I was also excited and surprised that he dropped to the 10th pick. The three receivers the Lions have are outstanding, and should score a lot of points if Charles Rogers stays healthy and our QB can get them the ball. As much as I have given up on this team, I have to say that they should win 9 or 10 games and get to the playoffs this year. It is a realistic goal. The pressure is on Harrington and Mariucci at this point. Most of the pressure is on Mariucci, since Garcia will be the QB if Joey can't get it done. If only we didn't have to play the games – we always look better on paper!

The yearly cycle of a Lion fan is very interesting. It is like the mourning process itself. The hope of life is there from draft day in April through the first game in September. As the games are played and the reality of the Lions history repeats itself, depression sets in. After the depression initially, the anger comes out at mid season when it becomes obvious that we will have the same results. After the season, the anger holds on from December through March – it goes along with the dreariness of our cold, bleak winters in Detroit. When April arrives, the hope of spring, better weather and draft day erases the pain we have struggled with since September. The cycle repeats itself every year for the Lions' fan.

The talk about the Lions has been non-stop for the past four days since the draft. This town is absolutely crazy about NFL football. Some people say that we are crazy for the Lions. I'm not so sure about that. If anything, we are crazy because of the Lions! The Pistons are in the playoffs with an excellent chance at repeating as NBA Champions, and 90% of the talk is about the Lions.
I have become one of the fans again that is really looking forward to September. I may never give up on this team; I think it's because we know what it might feel like should we ever win the championship. Without question, it would be the biggest sports thrill of my life, and that of millions of Lions fans throughout the country.

Almost a week after the draft, the Lions talk continues on the sports shows. The question today was "Should Matt Millen be given a new contract after his expires this year." Most people said yes, because of the excitement of the recent draft day. There is a feeling that he has done a great job the past few years in the draft. The one that might cost him his job was the Harrington draft four years ago. After this week, I'm sure things will die down until training camp in July. We open at home against the Packers, play the Bears on the road and then have a bye in week three. We should know by then if Harrington will be the guy during week four, or Garcia will be put in to take over. The Lions are one of the great things about fall in Michigan.

The Lions talk continues. Spindler says the only acceptable outcome this season is the team making the playoffs, and winning a playoff game. I agree. Making the playoffs is simply not good enough. What might be equally important to fans is starting to play exciting football again. Aside from all the losing, the games have been almost unwatchable. When Barry Sanders played, games were exciting whether we won or lost. The Lions talk might die down as the draft is one week removed, and the Pistons get further into their championship run.

The Lions had their mini-camp this past weekend, with all the draft choices in. This is Super Bowl week in Detroit. That's all you see and hear about on sports shows is the improved team the Lions have this year. Roy Williams made a spectacular catch with one hand; the ball was under thrown and he caught it with his one hand and trapped it on his back. It was an amazing catch. Shut it down for the season, this is as good as it might get. No one of course mentioned that Joey completely under threw the ball and it was a terrible pass! We will see what kind of coach Steve Mariucci is.

They are still talking Lions on the sports radio stations around Detroit, two weeks after the NFL draft. The question to the fans was which of the three young receivers will have the best year; Charles Rogers, Roy Williams or Mike Williams. Most people thought it would be Roy Williams. People just love to talk NFL football in Detroit and all over the United States. I believe that football has become the national past time, taking over baseball.

It is May 12, 2005, and Matt Millen is considering making an offer to Ty Law, the ex U of M all pro cornerback, who has championship rings with the Patriots. He is recovering from foot surgery, but Millen feels you can't have too many cornerbacks. We will see if we can land him; I'm thinking the Patriots let him go for reasons beyond the salary cap. I can't wait until August when the pre-season games begin. There will be a great deal to write about this season; I think the boys will give me enough material to finish this book. If the season goes poorly, as most of the last 48 have, then there will be many more "I don't believe it' moments to write about. I hope the luck and history of this franchise turns around, so I can write about the miracles of the 2005-2006 season!

There was a leak on the sports radio show about a contest that was completed this past week by EA sports for a skills competition to be aired on July 16, 2005. Joey Harrington was one of seven quarterbacks in the competition; guess which place he came in? Last place – seventh out of seven quarterbacks. And the quarterbacks were not the top quarterbacks in the NFL. No Culpeper, Farve, Brady, Vic or Manning. Joey comes in last! Could that be connected to the Lions 16-48 record the last four years? A funny piece on Harrington recently suggested that he change his name from Joey, to Joe. This might inspire an image of greater leadership. He wasn't 'Joey' Namouth, or 'Joey' Montana or 'Joey' Schmitt.

❖❖❖

The odds are out for the 2006 Super Bowl. The Lions are 42:1 odds to win the Super Bowl this year. The sports radio show pointed out that every one of the NFL teams are considered a better chance to win it including the top seven college teams! Of course, the Lions probably don't have the worst odds; some team is probably 100:1. We never get any respect around the country.

Big news! Charles Rogers was allowed to take off his red shirt and put on a blue shirt. This means he can take contact during the mini camps. The red shirt indicated that he was not to be hit due to the concern of his two broken collar bones the last two seasons. This was discussed on sports radio off and on throughout the day.

Chapter 6

The top 20
'I Don't Believe It's' since 1970

There are so many "I Don't Believe It Moments" it was hard to narrow it to the top 20. Some of these are not really "moments"; but are amazing records or streaks that the Lions have had. Anyway, here is my top 20 since 1970:

20. The Eagles beat the Lions 58-37 in the first round of the playoffs after Lomas Brown guaranteed a victory. Philadelphia led 51-7 at one point. Rodney Peete, the ex-Lion throws for three TD"s going 17-25 for 270 yards; Dec. 30, 1995.

19. 16 game losing streak to the Redskins in the 80's and 90's

    It is hard to believe you can lose that many in a row to one team; but the Redskins were great in those days.

18. 13 game losing streak to the Vikings in the 70's

    Here is another team that found every possible way to beat the Lions. You could have 20 "I Don't Believe It" moments, just with the Vikings.

17. Bears win on opening kickoff of overtime; fastest end in NFL history - 1980

Everyone remembers this one – I think it was a Thanksgiving Day game.

16. Lawrence Taylor's 97 yard interception return for a TD – 1982

Detroit was about to score from the three yard line, and then in a flash, it was over.

15. Sterling Sharpe TD catch uncovered losing a playoff game to the Packers - 1993

We had just beaten the Packers the week before at home to end the season. Not a good time for a blown coverage; Sharpe didn't have a Lion defender within 20 yards of him.

14. Two point attempts in Arizona by Bobby Ross down 23-19 - 1999

He tried two, 2 point conversions, saying he didn't want to play for overtime because of the heat in Arizona.

13. Reggie Brown almost dies on the field against the Jets; the same day Barry Sanders rushes for over 2000 yards – Dec. 21, 1997.

Was I really watching a second Lion die on the field? A strange game of highs and lows; Sanders over 2000 yards, Brown's medical crisis and the Lions clinching the playoff spot.

12. Marty takes the wind in overtime in Chicago - 2001

I was stunned to see him give the Bears the ball; even with a huge wind. I had never seen that in an NFL game. Has it ever happened before or since?

11. 23-20 loss to Chicago preventing playoffs; Edinger field goal; start of Millen era - 2000

    Charlie Batch re-injured his ribs at the end of the game. The Bears took great satisfaction keeping us out of the playoffs. Edinger was the kicker from Michigan State – how ironic.

    Batch said that if he didn't get hurt that game, Millen may have never come in, and he may not have signed with the Steelers walking away with a ring for Super Bowl XL in Detroit.

10. 23-20 loss to Tampa Bay – "What's a guy gotta do to get fired around here" - 1988

    Again, this loss kept us out of the playoffs. Darryl Rogers says one of the boldest things I have ever heard in sports.

9. Eddie Murray misses a FG against the 49'ers preventing NFC championship - 1983

    We all remember Monte Clark praying to the heavens. When Murray missed wide right, it was a sick feeling. We had a golden opportunity to play in the NFC championship game.

8. 5-0 playoff loss at Dallas - 1970

    I loved Greg Landry and Lem Barney. This was one of the best teams we have had the past 50 years. We remember the safety – we should have won that game.

7. A fan is roughed up at Ford Field holding a "Fire Millen" sign - 2005

    I was at this one but left before all the commotion. I saw it on the news. This day will be remembered as one of the most embarrassing and worst in Lion's history.

6. Botched snap – missed extra point against the Vikings - 2004

I will never forget this one! When it happened, I went to my computer and began writing this book.

5. Mike Utley is paralyzed at the Silver dome

What a sad day in Lion's history. It shows how dangerous this NFL game is. I am surprised more players don't get paralyzed with the speed of the game and the level of violent collisions. Mike Utley has been a very courageous man making progress with his mobility, and raising money and awareness for patients with spinal cord injuries. We will never forget his 'thumbs up' as he was carried off the field that day.

4. Barry Sanders retires - 1999

My disappointment and disbelief over this was intense. It was not only the end of an era we may never see again, but I so wanted to see Barry break the all time rushing record. He had so much respect for Walter Payton, that he did not want to displace him. Playing for the Lions has also taken it's toll on him. That is understandable. It can destroy an athletes' energy.

3. 24 game road losing streak from 2000-2003

Absolutely amazing! It was hard to believe that the Lions could lose every road game played for three straight years. I think this record may stand forever.

2. Chuck Hughes death on the field at Tiger Stadium - 1971

This was the saddest day in the history of Lions football. The only time a player has died on the field during an NFL game. I remember hearing about his death when I got home from the game on TV.

1. 63 yard field goal by Tom Dempsey - 1970

    This book starts out with this memory watching the game at my buddy Al's house in Detroit.

When we saw the ball go through to win the game for New Orleans, the title of my book was born; "I Don't Believe It."

Chapter 7

The 2005 season diary - 'Can You Believe It'?

Should it be Joey or Jeff? After two exhibition games of the 2005 pre-season, most are saying Joey since he is 15 of 16 with a quarterback rating of 107. I say Jeff, because he has led the team on its only touchdown and he has a great ability to escape a rush and can run. We will see by game four of the regular season. The young receivers look great; Rogers is healthy. The defense looks bad; the team looks like the same old Lions, but it's hard to say during the pre-season.

It's Monday night football against the Rams in the pre-season; Al Michaels, John Madden, and our new black jerseys. Big time in the motor city – our Lions get to showcase their new team, and the stadium which will host Super Bowl 40. The starters should play two or three quarters. Next February, will we be able to say, "I don't believe it, the Lions are in the Super Bowl?" I don't think so; but it would be the ideal ending for this book.

37-13 Rams on Monday night pre-season; and "it was worse than that" as the morning sports talk show described the game. I guess the Lions weren't "ready for some football." I was at this masterpiece, and when I saw the Lions coming onto the field through a cloud of smoke in their new black uniforms, I said I hoped that wasn't the highlight of the night. It was. The new uniforms were great – I like the look. The play on the field looked very familiar however. The third exhibition game is supposed to be the dressed rehearsal for the start of the season in two weeks; let's hope it doesn't reflect the ability of this team. John Madden would say that the Rams looked like they were playing against a "Pop Warner" team in this one.

The offense and defense were both horrible. Special teams played well. Let's review some of the highlights. The opening drive was a three and out. There were two incompletions by Harrington and a three yard run. The first play for the Rams was a 64 yard run. The Rams did whatever they wanted all night; receivers wide open – they ran at will. There were a lot of excuses after the game for Joey Harrington, because the offensive line played so poorly, resulting in at least four sacks at key times. I don't want to hear the excuses; I do not believe Harrington has what it takes to lead this team and be successful. He is similar to Darko Milichek of the Pistons; a very high draft choice that is probably going to be a bust. His three and out got the team off to a very bad start. Later, in the red zone, the Lions run the ball in for a TD but were flagged for not one but two holding penalties. Back to the 25 yard line; Harrington makes two throws on second and third down. The first was three yards and incomplete and the second was seven yards and dropped by Pollard. They did not even attempt to throw the ball into the end zone. Is that Harrington or Mariucci? At a key point in the game, we go for it on fourth down and half a yard when the score was 21-6. A touchdown puts us right back in the game. They run right up the middle fooling no one, and we lose a yard and turn the ball over on downs. Was that Mariucci or Harrington? Was it Tollner or Harrington?

In the third quarter, Garcia takes over at QB; I am looking forward to him proving me right with my buddy who I tell is the better of the two quarterbacks. His first play results in two Lion penalties; illegal receiver down field and intentional grounding! I can't take this anymore! "I don't believe it!"

We shouldn't over react to this loss. I liked how the players handled it after the game, and I thought Mariucci handled it well also when he said that he was "alarmed' by the performance. He should be alarmed. I do not have much confidence in our head coach. He is clearly a very well spoken, likable guy, but has not been effective in his first two years here. I still believe that Garcia will end up as the starter, because he sees the field better and runs well at key times. Harrington has no touchdowns in three games; not a good sign. Our back up QB's have both thrown TD passes with the second and third units in.

My friend and I even commented on all the other things that went wrong on this night; a serious neck injury to a Ram player delaying the game for 20 minutes; the over hanging camera coming down on the field and having to be corrected; and the offensive statistics being added wrong for both teams at half time. When dealing with the Lions, you never know what to expect. Well, you know not to expect championship football since 1957, don't you?

❖❖❖

I think everyone is over estimating the talent that Matt Millen has brought to the team. Or, the coaching and quarterbacking is so poor that it destroys any talent that we may be able to show. They are an interesting team; you can't be surprised if they win 9 or 10 games; and you can't be surprised if they win five or six games. We will start the story September 11th against the Packers. A Packer fan held a sign at last night's game saying, "you're going down Lions on Sept' 11th – The Messenger." We will soon find out.

The last exhibition game in Buffalo – a disaster; Jeff Garcia breaks his leg! I thought he was the best quarterback on the team. They are in trouble now. Some of my friends with season tickets are not optimistic. One guy says "I'm giving up my season tickets after this year if they don't make the playoffs." The Lions actually won the game and looked good. The third string (now second string) quarterback, Dan Orlovsky, played quite well for a rookie. He looks like he has good potential. It comes down to two key people to determine the success of the year; Joey Harrington and Steve Mariucci. If things don't go well, it could get ugly at Ford Field. I will be there Sunday when they open the season against the Packers. God help us!

While on the internet I noticed an article on the most valuable teams in the NFL. Being curious, I found the Lions listed at #18 out of 32 teams. A 44% ranking compared to the value of all other teams – that's just about the same as their winning percentage the past 49 years. I was surprised that the value wasn't higher. The Washington redskins were #1 and the Minnesota Vikings were last at #32. I have to do something with my time while I wait for the big season opener!

Three days until the opener. I will be there with my buddies. I'm not as excited as I used to be, probably because I don't expect much out of the Lions this year. I am predicting an 8-8 season this year. The older I get (I am turning 50 this year), the less into sports I am. As a young man, I had a sense of ease about life; a sense that life was simple. As I experienced some of the more difficult things about adult life, my perspective on the importance of sports changed. Becoming a father, going through two divorces, and managing a career over 25 years, has changed me. I understand what is really important in life. Sport are not one of those things. That doesn't mean that I don't get pleasure in losing myself in sports; I still do. It's just on a different level. I am a huge pro basketball fan – very passionate about our Pistons. It's because they recently won a championship. I'm sure if the Lions ever got that good, I would be a crazy fan again. I think part of it is that I really believe I am facing reality with the Lions and accept the strong possibility they will never be good until ownership is changed.

The Lions earn a 17-3 victory over the Packers on September 11, 2005. You must give the Lions, Harrington and the defense credit for this win. Harrington was steady with two TD passes, no interceptions and a rating in the 90's. The defense was the best I have seen it in years. Kennedy's Interception tip to Holt was fantastic. The pass coverage was excellent. The Lions got a huge break that changed the game when a completion on a bomb down to the Lions' three yard line was called back for offensive pass interference. On that play, the Packers top receiver went down for the year with an ACL injury. If they score that touchdown to tie the game, there was a very real risk of losing.

The headlines in the paper said "Undefeated"; "Super Bowl or Bust"! We need to wait a moment – aren't we over reacting just a little bit? There is one little problem with this optimism – there are 15 games left to be played. Last year's 4-2 start ended ugly, losing 8 of the last 10 games. Why don't we wait until they play half of their games before we get too excited? This team has ripped my heart out many times; I have learned to be cautious. On the other hand, the optimism is warranted. The Lions looked better than they have in a long time. Their division is weak, so there is a legitimate chance of winning the North. Are my delusions coming back again?

❖❖❖

Back to reality in game two; "Can't Bear to watch!, Lions clawed 38-6," "Lions mauled by Bears 38-6." On the sports radio show they are having callers spin "the wheel of Lions' mediocrity." It was another horrible performance that looked a lot like the pre-season loss to the Rams a few weeks ago on Monday night football. The trouble began when our substitute kicker, Remy Hamilton from U of M, missed an extra point after a nice TD pass from Harrington to Roy Williams which appeared to tie the game at seven. His one moment in the NFL at age 31, and he can't convert an extra point. I guess his NFL career will be considered a disappointment. Everything caved in from there. A 73 yard punt return for a touchdown; an interception return for a touchdown; five Harrington interceptions; 28 yards rushing by the Lions compared to 186 by the Bears. Once again, the Lions make Kyle Orton look like a seasoned pro in his second game in the NFL. The two other moments that stand out were when Roy Williams turned the wrong way on a pattern in the end zone, resulting in an easy interception for Chicago. When he got to the bench, he got into a shouting match with Kevin Jones. The final symbolic straw was when the Lions go for it on fourth and one in the second half, and Harrington and Jones collide on the handoff losing three yards. One of the sports shows said it best; "you look for consistency and improvement and we see neither in this team."

Now I said I won't judge Harrington and the Lions until they have played eight games this year, and I am sticking to that promise. The Bears looked very good, and they may be the best team in the North this year. I must say at this point though that our offensive line is terrible. They don't open holes in the run game, and they give Joey two seconds to throw the ball. I challenge anyone to find a worse line in the NFL. This division may be won this year with seven or eight wins, which means you are always in it in the North. The problem is, even if the Lions win the division with 7-9 wins and go to the playoffs, they will get killed in the first round. I still cannot believe that Mr. Ford gave Millen a five year extension to be the Lions president, after having the worst record in the NFL his first four years. I do believe at this point he will have no choice but to fire Mariucci if the team does not win at least seven games. Peter King of the national media noted that "Joey looked like a piranha on the sidelines," with no one going near him. He interpreted this to represent a lack of respect by teammates.

As an example of how crazy Detroit is about the NFL and the Lions, look no further than the sports talk shows the next day. "I can't take them anymore; they are terrible...." This after my alma-mater Michigan State had a huge win at Notre Dame Saturday, 44-41 in overtime, resulting in their national ranking of number 17 this week in college football. They eventually got to that game after an hour of doom and gloom discussion about the "kittens."

On the cover of the NFL preview magazine the headlines read, "How the Lions' Won the Super Bowl" – in the "pigs fly" edition. The fan predictions for this year included the following: 1) 7-9 – There should still be a good receiver left when their drafting number 12 next year; 2) 9-7 – The Lions will sneak into the playoffs, where they will be annihilated 45-0. However, this will be seen as progress, and the

M&M boys will be rewarded with contract extensions; 3) 9-7 – the Lions will make the playoffs and lose. Any better than that and I'll eat my shorts; 13-3 – The season will culminate with a Super Bowl victory. Note: this prediction was made after taking a prescribed medication that has euphoria as a side effect; 4) 8-8 – Based on some lucky breaks, Super Bowl? They have about as much chance to play in it as I do.

The Lions have a bye in week three and will not play for two weeks until they travel to Tampa Bay October 2, 2005. Tampa is 2-0. Everyday on the sport talk shows you hear hours of Lion analysis. The offensive line, Harrington, the defense, the coaches, the draft picks... it never stops. People are obsessed with the NFL and Detroit is obsessed with the Lions. I am sure they will be discussed daily until they play their third game. These two weeks will seem to take forever. I am looking forward to the next chapter with the Lions. Will they continue their horrible play, or reverse things in the right direction? History would suggest the latter; but you never know!

Our Lions are all alone in first place at 1-1; how about that! Chicago had to play a real NFL team this week in the Bengal's, and got their asses kicked 24-7. The Vikings finally won, beating the Saints 33-16; and the Packers go to 0-3 by losing to the Bucs 17-16. The other three North teams are 0-3, 1-2 and 1-2. The record for the North is 3-8. There is no question in my mind that nine wins will take the division; most likely eight wins, with an outside shot at seven. Could six wins take this division? It seems impossible, but you never know. These are four bad football teams. The Lions are already a six point underdog at Tampa this Sunday.

There are three days before Sunday and the third game of the season. Not as much talk on the radio this week about the Lions because of the Michigan/Michigan State game on Saturday. After this weekend, the sports radio shows will once again be filled with Lions talk. Jeff Garcia will probably be able to play by the sixth game of the season. If Harrington has played poorly, I'm sure he will be the starter. It is difficult to know if Garcia has what it takes to win. The Lions have so many weaknesses; quarterback is just one of them. The biggest problem for this team is the offensive line and the coaching. I'm going to see the game on my girlfriends' dad's new 62" high definition TV. I wonder if they will look better on a high tech screen.

They still look bad, even on a great TV. Actually, the Lions gave a very solid effort – the defense was great except for two big TD passes. The offense was horrible until the last four minutes of the game, when Harrington led the team down the field and threw an apparent game winning touchdown. Was Pollard in bounds? "I don't believe it"; the play is reversed by the re-play official and the Lions lose. I thought he was out of bounds on the re-play they showed – later that night, in slow motion it was clearly a touchdown – the Lions got screwed! They should be 2-1 instead of 1-2. The other horrible play was a defensive holding by Goodman that reversed an interception by Detroit. Two bad calls by the officials that both went against the Lions. Tampa wins 17-13 over Detroit. Tampa had four turnovers and we still couldn't beat them. The Lions had 145 yards of offense and only six first downs going into the last drive in the fourth quarter with just over five minutes left in the game.

◆◆◆

On the NFL show they had a comedy skit about the NFC North division. They said the NFL rules would be changed for them, and would let them end a play by two hand touch on defense. They said that if you could spell Mariucci's name correctly, you could be the Lions quarterback. The last dig said that Detroit gets to bring real Lions on the field with them for games. Our division is bad; 3-10 as of today. And two of the wins were against each other!

I am actually starting to feel bad for Harrington. The kid looked so depressed after this game. Even when he does something right, it doesn't go his way. It is clear that Garcia will be the QB in three weeks when he gets healthy, although that will not guarantee success either. The good news is that the Lions are tied for first with Chicago at 1-2. I really believe that the winner of the North will have 6-8 wins. I will be surprised if any team has nine or more.

Green Bay goes to 0-4 and the North is now 3-11 this year. More good news for the Lions; Charles Rogers, the second pick in the draft three years ago, has been suspended for four games due to drug use. It was the third test he has failed. What else can go wrong for the Lions? You know there will be more.

❖❖❖

The Lions beat Baltimore 35-17 on October 9, 2005, to go to 2-2 for the year. I was out of town on a golf trip (where I got my first hole in one) so I didn't see the game. Baltimore had 21 penalties which was the second highest total in NFL history. Our defense played very well. Harrington was 10-23 for 97 yards with one TD and two interceptions. It was another poor performance by Joey. I am sure that as soon as Garcia is recovered from his leg injury, he will be the starter for the Lions. That should be three games from now in Cleveland.

On talk radio this week, one of the topics was if Mariucci should be fired. I find this strange the week after they won a game. The truth is the Lions should be 3-1 if they were not robbed by an official's call in Tampa Bay. They are in first place in their division; Chicago is 1-3, Minnesota is 1-3 and Green Bay is 1-4. Our division is 5-12 overall. The other big story is our receiver Roy Williams making negative comments obviously directed to Harrington. The shows are making fun of the Lions playing music from "Days of Our Lives." I am surprised there is so much controversy the week after a win. It must be that a lot of people, including the players are not fooled by their first place position. Everyone seems to be waiting for a typical Lions collapse. Will it come, or maybe the question is when will it begin?

❖❖❖

"Oh my," as Mark Champion used to say; Carolina 21-20 over the Lions with a TD pass with 32 seconds left. The kick is returned by McQuarters to the 50 yard line, but Joey goes 0-4 passing and cannot get the team to the 35 yard line for a chance to win. It was pathetic. On a day when the defense hit harder than I have seen a Lions team hit in 20 years; get four turnovers including two TD returns off of interceptions, and they still lose. It was as though we had no offense on the field. The defense outscores the offense 14-6. I thought the best idea was to refuse the ball on offense and force Carolina to play offense the whole game. Even though Harrington threw for over 200 yards, which is a big day for him, I believe his career is over as a Lion. As soon as Garcia is ready which should be two weeks, the change will be made.

The talk shows continue to play the theme song from the "Days of our Lives" soap opera, calling it 'the days of the Lions.' Joey apologized to the team, and they played the sound bite all day with him saying "sorry." The coaches and offensive line are terrible. Joey had no time to throw, and when he did he had trouble throwing the ball. When the game was on the line, they failed; "this team doesn't believe it can win." I heard Dan Miller call the last play that went incomplete and ended the game – the same depressed voice we heard from Mark champion for years, without the "holy mackerel." What is really amazing is that the Lions are two plays away from being 4-1 this year instead of 2-3. The soap opera continues next week in Cleveland for our first place Lions. The North division is 0-9 on the road this year.

There were two interesting statistics that tell you everything you need to know about this past game. The Lions offense had a negative two yards on their last 10 plays of the game and the defense, which had given up only four first downs to Carolina through three quarters, gave up 10 fourth quarter first downs. The talk about Harrington will not stop. He will probably play his last game as a starter this weekend in Cleveland. Good luck Joey!

A quote from Harrington in the paper; "They will not bring me down." I have to give him credit – he seems to take all the hatred from fans and negative comments from the media and other players, and keeps going forward. He is a very well thought of, nice guy. I guess when you have been paid 25 million dollars for five years, it can toughen you up. Garcia is getting half of the reps in practice this week – he will clearly get his chance in the next few weeks. The Lions soap opera continues!

It is John Joseph Harrington's 27th birthday today. What a present he might receive from his boss – being benched in favor of Jeff Garcia. We should probably call him J.J. instead of Joey. The only thing you can predict about the Lions is that in the end, it will be bad! Fans can't wait for the soap opera to continue Sunday at Cleveland.

❖❖❖

Joy in Lion town! Detroit beats Cleveland 13-10 to go to 3-3 and stay in first place tied with Chicago. Mariucci makes the switch to Garcia and he played great. He ran for a touchdown, completed about 66% of his passes throwing for 210 yards with no interceptions. And the key was making the big play at the right time. It looked totally different than Harrington. I think Joey can see the writing on the wall – he won't get back in this year unless Garcia gets hurt.

The bad news was that the Lions had three severe injuries to key players. With the Lions, you learn early that you cannot have good news without some bad thrown in. A key receiver tore his Achilles and is out for the year. Our two best defensive players were also hurt – Shawn Rogers with a knee that could keep him out for the year or at least a month; and Dre' Bly our top corner who dislocates his wrist by running into his own man. It was Bly who was covering Charles Rogers in practice the first time he broke his collar bone two years ago. Hard to say how long he will be out or if surgery will be necessary. This has got to give the team a big lift watching a guy who has the leadership ability and the skills to give them a chance. With Joey, it was like we had no offense.

◆◆◆

It's October 30, 2005, and the Bears beat the Lions 19-13 in overtime on an interception returned for a touchdown thrown by Jeff Garcia. Its Halloween day and the radio sports shows are playing sounds of people screaming and shrieking when the Lion offense is mentioned. I went to the game instead of golfing on one of the last beautiful days in the Detroit area (67 degrees); a bad choice. My good buddy offered me a free ticket down near the field. Just before the last play of the game, my friend says to me, "I can't watch this anymore," referring to the Lions offense. He suggested it as the new title to this book.

The final statistics were better than I thought. Garcia was 23-35 for 197 yards. We must have run for 100 yards. The offense is so boring that it really is hard to watch. The defense is playing well giving up only 13 points. You should win a game when the defense allows 13 points. Garcia was rushed and blitzed constantly never having more than two seconds to throw the ball. Our offensive line is the biggest problem on the team without question. We were also frustrated by our defense never blitzing. Our coordinator doesn't believe in it. It was a Bear's blitz that won the game for them when the Lions were on the Bear's 37 yard line with two minutes left in regulation. Garcia was sacked at the 45 yard line taking them out of field goal range.

Mariucci has the same depressing speech after the game. He refuses to change the offense; refuses to direct the defensive coordinator to blitz occasionally, and has not been able to put together an effective offensive line. I think we should take another receiver in the first round next year! I do not think he is a very effective coach. He is now 14-25 as the head coach of the Lions. And Millen is now 19-52 as the President of the team in four and a half years. I'm starting to get to the point I did last year when I was rooting for the Lions to lose. Of course they won that game against Arizona. They happen to play Arizona in two weeks from now. Will I root against them again? I think I need to see my therapist. The Lions illness is returning and I find myself dazed and confused.

◆◆◆

The sports talk shows say "it's Groundhog Day all over again." The Vikings win 27-14 over the Lions. This one was over when the Vikings scored 21 points in just over three minutes of the second quarter. Joey helped them out of course with a fumble and an interception deep in Lions' territory on consecutive possessions. Even though Harrington through for almost 300 yards and completed 60% of his passes, he continued to look lost and ineffective.

Mariucci left Charles Rogers home for the game after returning from a four week drug suspension. They said he was rusty from the lay off and did not have a good week of practice. I find it amazing that they bring a guy from the taxi squad for the game and leave home the guy who was drafted second overall four years ago. Rogers must have really pissed off his coach.

The wheels are starting to come off. You can see this season slipping away. If Garcia can return and be effective the rest of the way, I could see them winning four or five games of their final eight. If he is not effective, they will be lucky to win three more. I don't understand playing Harrington yesterday. After benching him for Garcia two weeks ago, and all but saying his career was over in Detroit, they put him back in. It was obvious the Lions had no chance of winning that game with Harrington at quarterback. Why they did not start the rookie Orlovsky makes no sense to me. What's the worse he could do, lose? He might have given them a chance to win. With Harrington we had no chance.

They showed Matt Millen watching the game from a private box. He looked disgusted and ready to kill someone. I think he sees the writing on the wall. He is going to have to fire Mariucci if things don't change the in next two months. The only question is do you keep Harrington under a new coach or let him go also? How Millen has kept his job is beyond me. Chuck Schmitt who was the general manager before Millen must be getting some quiet satisfaction out of this.

Watching the game was an interesting experience for me. I began watching with no hope of winning this game. It was actually a relief. No disappointment about the end result – I totally expected it. This was against a Viking team that has been a laughing stock in the league to this point, and one that just lost their quarterback for the season to a knee injury. It is strange watching your team as a casual observer – it has become a professional obligation in order to finish this book. Throughout most of the second half, I was turning to the PGA golf tournament to see if Tiger would win another one. They are so predictable, so bad and so boring that they are hard to watch. My friend said it all the week before, "I can't watch this anymore."

Roy Williams said he was supposed to play 20-30 plays in the game. Was it a miscommunication between him and his coach, or a message from Mariucci to Williams? Mariucci supposedly asked Roy if he could go in when Mike Williams was injured and he said "no." I don't think Mariucci liked that. He is trying to send a message to his young, spoiled receivers who have performed far under their expectations.

A radio show this week said that Bill Ford Sr. will not get rid of Millen – he likes him too much, and that is more important than winning. The host called for Millen to do the honorable thing and resign after the season. Although I see his point, it's a little hard to walk away from a job that pays you five million dollars a year. As Darryl Rogers said, "what's a guy got to do around here to get fired?"

The Lions are at home this week against Arizona. If they lose this game, the wheels have officially come off and the season is over. We don't know if Garcia is healthy enough to play. It makes no sense to play Harrington. I hope they consider the rookie Dan Orlovsky. They play at Dallas the next week, and home to Atlanta on Thanksgiving Day. I don't see them having much of a chance to win either of those, so they could be 4-7 at that point if they beat Arizona.

It is so frustrating! Many of my friends including myself are not renewing our season tickets anymore. What is the point? We have to accept that this is going to be a losing franchise until the Fords no longer own the team. I heard that since he has owned the team the Lions have had 13 winning seasons since 1964. 29 losing seasons since 1964 – no wonder Lion fans are discouraged and struggling with mental illness from September through December each year! And after the NFL season we get to look forward to a long, cold winter. Thank god for the Red Wings and Pistons.

❖❖❖

The Lions beat Arizona in the ninth game 29-21 to go to 4-5. I even bet that we would cover the four point spread. Harrington was very good, throwing for three TD's and 0 interceptions. His QB rating was close to 120. Roy Williams, who is by far our best receiver, caught all three TD's. We had a good running game as well. There is only one problem with this win. It was against one of the worst teams in the NFL; and Arizona had the ball with one minute to go with a chance to tie!

The reason I am not excited about this win is that I had given up on the season weeks ago. I looked at the Lion's record to this point after nine games. Their four wins have come against teams with a combined record of 9-27; their five losses are against teams with a combined record of 28-16. Does that explain why they have no chance this year?

They are playing at Dallas next week; no chance. Home for Thanksgiving against Atlanta; a 30% chance of winning. Home against Minnesota - 50% chance; at Green Bay – a 30% chance. Home to Cincinnati – a 20% chance; At New Orleans – a 50% chance. Their last game is at Pittsburgh – no chance. They will win two to three more games and end up either 6-10 or 7-9. The Bears have won five in a row now and will win the division with at least nine wins. It is very possible the Lions will win only one more game and end at 5-11. Their final record has a lot to do with if Garcia is healthy enough to play; with him I say they win three more – if it's Harrington I say they win one more.

Seven games left in the season. It is another season of hope all but gone. Why are Lions fans' so naïve when it comes to their team? History has shown us that we are not very good. We are envious of other cities with great NFL teams; New England, Denver, San Francisco, Dallas, Green Bay, New York, Indianapolis and Washington. All are teams that have won championships over the past 20 years. I believe Indianapolis will win this year.

The wheels are about to come off; there is no chance they will win both of their next two games – there is a 30% chance they will win one of the two. I believe they will lose both and go to 4-7. Watch all hell break loose if that happens. I hope I am wrong.

❖❖❖

Dallas 20-7 over Detroit. The Lions get 18 penalties – the most since 1970. The penalties result in nine Dallas first downs – the second most in NFL history. I found myself rooting for five more penalties so they could set the all time record. Actually, the refs made several questionable calls against Detroit. One of the penalties actually saved Detroit a touchdown, when Dallas picked off a Harrington pass and returned it for a TD. We were flagged for illegal procedure. The defense played hard considering half of the starters were out. Harrington looked decent, throwing downfield several times. Roy Williams and Charles Rogers also looked good. But once again, we will have to wait until next year for the playoffs. The Bears are now 7-3 having won their last six in a row. Detroit is 4-6 and is four games behind Chicago with six left to play.

So another year wasted. It will be interesting to see what changes are made; the most obvious one needed is a new coach. They may get rid of Charles Rogers. I think it is worth seeing Harrington one more year under a new system. It seems the defense has some great potential next year. There needs to be work on the offensive line – I hope they use their first draft pick here. Will the Fords clean house again and say goodbye to Millen? I doubt it.

In doing research for the book, I discovered that the Lions have averaged only 6.6 wins per year since 1970. That puts them in 27th place out of 32 teams. Miami has the most wins since 1970 averaging 9.65 wins per year. Only New Orleans, Atlanta, Arizona, Tampa Bay and Houston averaged fewer wins per year.

No wonder fans are having nervous breakdowns over this team at an all time rate. Our average season is either 7-9 or 6-10. The four times we won 10 or more games since 1970 was due to one man; Barry Sanders.

Tomorrow is the big Thanksgiving game against Atlanta. The Falcons need the win at 6-4. The Lions can officially end their season with a loss. They will either be 5-6 or 4-7 after tomorrow. The big drama is who will start at quarterback. I'm guessing it will be Garcia. I believe there will be some significant changes after this year.

❖❖❖

The headlines says it all; "Stuffed, Mashed and Cranburied." For the third straight time on national television, the Lions disgrace themselves and the city; Atlanta 27-7. Speculation after the game was that Mariucci would be fired the next day. Nothing happened. There are reports Jauron turned down the interim coach position the last five games. This team does not want to play for this coach. They quit on him a long time ago. You almost feel bad for Mariucci based on how depressed he looked after the game; but he is simply not a good coach. The $10 million pay out of his last two years will help him over the depression. Fans don't have that kind of fall back. A classic moment in this game; after a Lion receiver misses a pass in the end zone, he picks up the ball and throws it at 'Roary' the mascot. He is lying on the ground, when the ball hits him in the face. This is one of the most symbolic things I have seen representing the utter futility and frustration of this organization. The mascot takes one in the snout, from its own player! I wanted this picture for the front cover of the book, but thought the Lions might not give me permission.

The last five games are important for next year. You want to see what these young players have. I don't know why Millen just doesn't finish the season as head coach until they pick someone after the season. With four wins, we are the 10th worst team in the NFL. We don't even have much of a chance for the top five picks in the draft, and this year the top five are loaded. We should probably pick an offensive lineman anyway and not be seduced by the skill positions. Here we are just after Thanksgiving, and we are already talking about the draft in April. Such is the fate of a Lions fan!

Dan Miller of channel 2 sports first reported that the Lions brass may fire Mariucci after the Atlanta game. The Lions denied all reports – business as usual. Why not admit your mistake and move on; it's the Lions! Miller is in a strange position, as he was hired by the Lions to replace Mark Champion for the play by play on radio. I wonder how the Lions feel about his report.

I just heard that Charlie Sanders of the Lions came out with a book about the team this week. Darn, he beat me to it! It will be interesting to see if the book is a re-cap of his career with the Lions, or if he is critical about the last 48 years. I will read it for research. I am not giving up on this book. It is written by a fan, for the fans.

❖❖❖

Mariucci is gone! Now we have to work on Millen. How the Fords let him keep his job is amazing. It could have to do with Mr. Ford adopting Matt as his new son. We should call him Matt Ford! There are rumors that next year Ford will come out with its newest model, the "Millen." Millen has made three decisions on coaches over his five years here. He fired Gary Moeller (who would have been better than both guys he hired), and hired Mornhinwig and Mariucci. He clearly should not hire any other coaches whose last name begins with the letter "M". Too bad, because I would like to see them hire Mike Martz of the St. Louis Rams.

Dre' Bly then says that it is Harrington's fault that Mariucci was fired. He said that he has been a bad quarterback the entire time he played for the Lions. This shows you the lack of professionalism and problems that have existed on this team. If I were Harrington, I would punch him in the mouth in front of the team!

I am going to see them play Sunday against the Vikings. Will they play harder for Jauron? I think that they will. Olsen will call the offensive plays – Tollner was demoted and several coaches were also fired. They could essentially end the Vikings playoff hopes with a win. It's now time for these players to step up, act like professionals, and earn their paychecks.

They just named Garcia as the starting quarterback. This surprises me and may be the official end of Harrington in Detroit. You never know with the Lions. It could be they are starting Garcia because of the negative comments from Dre' Bly about Harrington. Garcia has maybe one or two years left in his career – he is certainly not a long term solution.

What more can you say about this team? The sports radio stations have been talking non-stop Lions all week. I may be going to the game this weekend against the Vikings. I would have been more interested in going if Harrington was starting. It's my chance to spend some time with my good friend. This is the last year I will pay for season tickets. The reality of this franchise has finally hit me. Will they get to the Super Bowl before I die? It's probably 50/50!

25 0f the 32 NFL teams have appeared in the Super Bowl. 17 of those 25 have a Super Bowl win. The six teams that have never been to the Super Bowl are Jacksonville, Cleveland, New Orleans, Arizona, Houston and Detroit. You really can't count Jacksonville that has been in the league 10 years and Houston that has been in the league four years.

Chapter 8

How the Lions compare to the rest of the NFL since 1970

As I said earlier, the Lions have averaged 6.6 wins per year since 1970, ranking them 27th out of 32 teams for average wins per season. The following are the average wins per season by team since 1970:

	Wins	Avg. wins/yr	Super Bowl appearances	Wins
1. Miami	338	9.65	5	2
2. Pittsburgh	332	9.20	6	5
3. Dallas	316	9.03	8	5
4. Minnesota	311	8.88	4	0
5. Denver	310	8.85	6	2
6. San Fran.	304	8.68	5	5
7. Oakland	304	8.68	5	3

8. Washington	301	8.60	5	3
9. St. Louis	290	8.28	3	1
10. Jacksonville	82	8.20	0	0
11. Baltimore	72	8.00	1	1
12. Kansas City	271	7.74	2	1
13. Philadelphia	271	7.74	2	0
14. Green Bay	267	7.63	4	3
15. New England	265	7.57	5	3
16. New York G.	265	7.57	3	2
17. Chicago	259	7.40	1	1
18. Tennessee	258	7.35	1	0
19. Buffalo	257	7.34	4	0
20. Seattle	214	7.33	1	0
21. Carolina	71	7.10	1	0
22. Cleveland	224	7.00	0	0
23. Indianapolis	243	6.94	2	1
24. Cincinnati	235	6.71	2	0
25. San Diego	234	6.70	1	0
26. New York J.	233	6.65	1	1

"I Don't Believe It!"

	Wins	Avg. wins/yr	Super Bowl appearances	Wins
27. Detroit	231	6.60	0	0
28. Atlanta	225	6.40	1	0
29. New Orleans	223	6.37	0	0
30. Arizona	215	6.14	0	0
31. Tampa Bay	172	5.93	1	1
32. Houston	16	5.30	0	0

Source: Sports Illustrated Football book of 2005.

Chapter 9

2005 - a mass nervous breakdown by fans; will we recover?

December 4, 2005; the wheels are really coming off. Fan uprising at Ford Field. The Lions were terrible again losing to the Vikings 21-16. They actually had a chance to win the game at the end, but a Garcia interception ended that. My buddy and I were so bored by the game we left in the middle of the third quarter. Garcia was awful and the offense was so boring, it was hard to watch.

Before the game I was outside and saw security staff collecting paper bags from fans, telling them they were not allowed inside. The bags were to be put over their heads as a symbol of being embarrassed by this team. The guard had about 10 bags in his hand. That was the first sign of the day that we were about to enter a place that had rules similar to old Russia. Fans in the second half began holding up signs saying "Fire Millen." One fan ran around the stadium with it and was eventually tackled by security. He was later told "never to come back to Ford Field again." This was all seen on Fox television. The bottom line is the Fords don't like criticism.

When Millen fired Mariucci last week, he said he must see the potential of the younger players. So what do the Lions do? They start a 35 year old quarterback who will not be with the team next year, and they do not dress Charles Rogers. That makes a lot of sense! You don't dress a guy who was the second overall pick in the draft four years ago, and is the fastest guy on the team. He has to "earn" playing time in practice. The second overall pick doesn't earn playing time – he is out there period. This decision shows that the Lions are getting rid of both Rogers and Harrington next year. I am happy for Harrington; he will probably be pretty good starting over with an organization that knows what they are doing.

❖❖❖

My buddy had a great idea for a fan protest at the last game in two weeks against the Bengal's. When the game starts, all the fans in the lower bowl get up and go to the concessions for 10 minutes, leaving all the seats empty. The television broadcast would certainly show the empty seats and comment about the frustration of Lions fans. I do believe that something noteworthy will take place at the last home game.

One of the sports radio stations is organizing the "angry man's march" outside Ford Field for the last game in two weeks. They are renting a billboard near the stadium to send a message to the Fords about the Lions. They will meet at one of the bars near the stadium and have asked fans to bring unused tickets to burn. This should be something to see. The message to the Fords is that he owns the team, but the Lions belong to the fans of Detroit!

Angry fan week continues on the sports radio shows. Today, the theme is "adopt an NFL team." Vote for the Bengal's, Colts, Broncos have been called in. All the problems this team has, gives these shows great material. I'm sure it's not very funny for the players. Even though they make a lot of money, this tail spin cannot be any fun. I really have no idea what it feels like to play at this level in a losing situation. At least NFL players pick up that big check to help lift their spirits; I'm guessing it may be harder for college football players that play for the love of the game, pride of representing their schools, and of course the women!

I heard that Red Wing fans were holding up "Fire Millen" signs at the hockey game last night. I don't think that the Fords can do anything about that. I guess Red Wing management believes in free speech! The morning sports show was playing a game called "name that Millen debacle." It was when he said Mornhinwig was his guy on Dec. 31st, 2002 and then fired him to hire Mariucci a few weeks later. I can't really blame Millen for that one; that happens all the time when a better coach comes along.

There was talk today, Dec. 8, 2005, on the sports radio show that Mike Shanahan has had a falling out with the owner and might be available. He might be a good choice for our new general manager. I would say so, since he has won two Super Bowls. Maybe Millen offers him the head coaching job. A friend asked me the other day what I would do if I were the owner of the team. The truth is that I have no experience with football other than being a fan. The Fords have been owners for 42 years and Millen has been in football all of his life. They are supposed to know what their doing. But I told my friend I would try to hire away one of the top presidents in football. New England's, Pittsburgh's, Parcells from Dallas, Shanahan from Denver. We need someone with a proven track record. Millen had no track record. Mornhinwig had no track record; Mariucci had some track record but that was not enough. Who knows what to do with this god forsaken team? Help!

◆◆◆

I picked up a copy of the Detroit Free Press in December of 2005. The headlines read "When Will the Pain End?" There was a picture of Bill Ford Jr. next to it. Of course, I assumed it was an article on the Lions. It was actually about the 60,000 jobs being cut in the auto industry and the big three slipping to almost 50% of the auto market. I guess this is a little more serious than why the Lions are so bad. Football is just a game. This has to do with peoples' jobs and feeding their families. We do get a little too serious about football sometimes, don't we?

The Detroit Free Press story reads "Lions fan sells loyalty on eBay." The ad on eBay read "former Detroit Lions supporter looking for new NFL team." The highest bid stands at $20 as of today. This fan is convinced that the Lions will never win until ownership is changed. The other piece in this article told the story of an ex-Lion player, Darryl Sanders who quit the team in 1966 after three years with Detroit. He was the starting left tackle at the time. The team went 4-9-1 that year and Darryl got a lucrative business offer and retired from football. He felt the Lions had "no vision" and felt they would never be a winner under the Ford ownership. This man knows how to see the future, doesn't he? He says that the organization is very dysfunctional now, and always has been. There is no foundation and there never has been one. The title of this article was "Quitting Time" by Michael Rosenberg.

In an interview with Dick Stockton who worked with Millen when he was a television analyst, the question was asked, "did the fans get to Millen?" Stockton laughed so much, he could hardly speak. "It doesn't mean a thing to Matt Millen. "I'm not saying he doesn't care. He cares about the fans. He wants the franchise to do well." It is nice to know that Millen is probably laughing at us, the fans, while he dines with Mr. Ford weekly to discuss the state of the Lions. Wouldn't you love to be at one of those dinners? The truth is that the fans are tired of Millen and the Fords. We should have realized what Darryl Sanders came to accept in 1966.

❖❖❖

The Lions will be on national television tomorrow night in Green Bay. It will be around 18 degrees. I saw three Lions players interviewed about the game and the first thing each of them said was how cold it was going to be. Is that amazing! You wonder why this team is considered soft and has a record of 4-8. I am guessing their thoughts should be about the game and the need to beat the Packers. The Lions are a six point underdog in this game. The Packers are 2-10! Detroit has not won at Lambeau Field since 1991. They have lost 13 straight games there which ties them with Arizona for the longest losing streak in the NFL to one team.

The paper has an article today comparing the Lions to the L.A. Clippers of the NBA. They have been the joke of the league the last 25 years. They are finally good this year with a record of 13-5 presently. Elgin Baylor has been the general manager there for the past 20 seasons. Baylor recently wanted to thank his owner for sticking with him; "his faith, and incompetence – never waned." "The Lions are their NFL replica, a long litany of futility directly related to the counterproductive instincts of ownership." The Clippers have been to the playoffs only three times; they have had 20 top 10 draft picks in that time. Baylor's record with the Clippers since 1986 is 522-1,022 with three playoff appearances. Millen since 2001 is 20-56 presently with no playoff appearances. Will the Ford's give their adopted son a chance to run the team for 20 years? It's possible!

◆◆◆

The headlines read "night clubbed" after Detroit lost to the Packers 16-13 on Sunday night football. At least the team didn't disgrace themselves. But it was really the same old thing. No passing game; Garcia threw a few good balls, but was very ineffective. You knew it was going to be "the same old thing" when Detroit settled for two field goals inside the five yard line in the first eight minutes of the game. Our inability to score a touchdown in the red zone is unbelievable. It is hard to score when you have no passing game. In the fourth quarter with the game tied 13-13, the Lions go for it on fourth and one. I'm thinking, "why not kick the field goal and take a three point lead?" O.K., their 4-8, what's the difference if they go for it? After calling a time out to discuss the play, they run a quarterback sneak with Jeff Garcia! Garcia is 6' 1" and weighs 188 pounds – he looked like a feather getting blown backwards. You have to be kidding. Joe Thiesman said, "that's a horrible call." They had just run two plays with our running backs to the right of center which got stopped for no gain. The defensive lineman for Green Bay is about 365 pounds – one of the biggest guys you have ever seen – and they run right at him again! Jauron is a terrible coach and has no chance of remaining with the team. I never liked his refusal to blitz when he was the defensive coordinator.

The play of the game was when it appeared the Lions had a safety after missing the touchdown on fourth down. They tackled the Packer running back in the end zone, but the guy threw the ball forward. They first called a safety, and then reversed the call saying it was not intentional grounding. What made it even worse, was that the Packers were also called for holding which would be another reason to call a safety. The refs decided the holding did not occur in the end zone, even though replays showed it did. The Green Bay coach went crazy throwing a challenge flag. When the final decision was explained to Jauron, he accepted it like a sheep. No protest, no anger. We are the Lions; we accept things not going our way! Lions fans had "Fire Millen" signs in the crowd; one also said "don't arrest me" referring to the freedom of speech issue in 'old communist Russia', I mean Ford Field.

◆◆◆

I was actually rooting for the Lions to lose, because the more controversy, the better for my chances to finish this book and get it published. I actually shut the television off when it went to overtime. I was up late the night before and was tired, but also knew they would lose in overtime. I have never turned off a Lions game, let alone not watch the overtime. What is happening to me? Is this a sign of health?

A Local Detroiter runs a web site for Lions fans. He gets three million hits per month! That is unbelievable. He is calling for a protest at the last home game. He wants all Lions fans to wear orange, the color of the visiting Bengal's. It will be an interesting game to watch on national television. The sports radio show today says the collapse of the Lions this year has been "an implosion of biblical proportion."

In the Detroit Free Press today, December 13, 2005, there is an interesting article by Drew Sharp; "Curse just one more bad excuse." Roy Williams is interviewed and says "Is this team cursed?" He wasn't joking. "I've never been on a team where things go wrong all the time, like all the time." "Congratulations, Roy, you've officially become a Detroit Lion!" "A dazed and confused Dick Jauron didn't have any answers during his news conference." "Everybody has opinions on what's wrong, but I don't think that anybody knows. "Find me the person that knows – that knows exactly what's wrong. Find me that person."

"Never before has the connection between the product and the consumer been as poisonous as it is now. Williams expects it to get ugly at the Lions' home finale Sunday against Cincinnati." Roy Williams says "It can't go on forever." "Have you already forgotten what team you're talking about Roy?" "Who else but the Lions could have a safety reversed? Has that ever happened before in the NFL?" The refs could have saved time in Green Bay "by just explaining that they were enacting the Lions clause of the league rulebook, which says that any team incapable of helping itself doesn't warrant any assistance from the officials." "Everybody wants this season to end as quickly as possible." "It has taken two years, but Williams understands that the sins of the fathers become the burden of the sons."

The power rankings in the NFL show the Lions ranked 30th of 32 teams. Only San Francisco and Houston were lower. The statement for Detroit referred to Roy Williams recognizing that the team is "jinxed";" but things might be different if not for poor management and under performing players. It will be interesting at Ford Field Sunday with protestors outside the stadium and fans wearing orange shirts; the colors of the visiting Bengal's. I do not believe this is meant as disrespect to the players as much as it represents the fans anger towards Millen and the Fords. My buddy told me if the book would have been finished, I could have sold 1000 of them to people in the protest lines.

The Detroit Free Press had nothing on the fan revolt today. The Detroit News however had quite a bit written about the last home game this year Sunday, December 18, 2005. There is a picture of Millen with his head in a target of a dart board with a dart in his forehead. It reads "aiming for Millen." There have been pictures of the Pope and Sadaam Hussein holding "Fire Millen" signs. There is a feeling that what really has gotten the fans outraged was when security tackled the fan holding the "Fire Millen" sign at the last home game. Now, the Lions are saying they will allow signs at the last game if they do not obstruct other fans or if they are not 'offensive', whatever that means. At the last home game, the Lions found "Fire Millen" signs offensive.

The other picture of Millen is with him in a diaper with a Lions symbol on it, saying "It's time for a change." That is funny. The message being that Millen has crapped himself and made a complete 'mess' of the organization. They are organizing fans to wear orange shirts, the color of the visiting team. Dexter Jenkins of the Center for the study of Sports in Society at Northeastern University in Boston is quoted as saying that fans in Philadelphia, Boston and New York are "similarly frenetic over their teams." Jenkins believes that "the Lions fan revolt is a product of 21st century media." The internet, all the T.V. and radio sports stations available.

The concern the Lions executives have along with many fans, is that Sundays game not result in another black eye for the city of Detroit. Especially since the Super Bowl is here in less than two months. What happened with the Pistons/Pacers brawl last year added to the already negative image of the city of Detroit. We will see what happens this Sunday.

There was a contest in the Detroit Free Press today asking fans to complete the phrase, "Yes, going to a Lions game can be extremely painful, but it's still better than...." I thought the funniest response was "...accidentally being hit in the groin by a policeman's Taser as I speak with an obnoxious telemarketer on my cell phone while watching a snow plow crush my car for which I dropped comprehensive coverage yesterday during a search for my lost puppy along a blizzard-choked freeway with no hat or gloves on my way home from being fired; but not by much."

◆◆◆

Prior to the Cincinnati game the headlines read, "Teed Off," Lions jerseys available reading "SUPER BOWLS" with a 0 underneath. Another one reading "REBUILDING SINCE 57." Predictions of a pro wrestling atmosphere are being made for Sunday's game. One caller said he would run naked onto the field! There is talk of a revolt. The bill board from the radio station 1130 will read "Not this MILLENium. Rebuilding since 57." Many fans were saying that they didn't care about the game anymore, they wanted to see the side show – the circus of chaos. An article from the Free Press said "if you want to make a statement to the Fords, stay away." A sign at the last home game read, 'Another Ford Recall.'

A day before the last home game against the Bengal's; headlines in the Free Press read, "Lions curious about approaching circus." One of the Lions players says he has never seen anything like this before. "We want to win as much as they want us to win." "We are not going out there to lose." "It's just disappointing that our fans are like that because I'm telling you, one day we're going to turn this thing around and it's all going to be in the past." I think we have heard that a few times in the past 48 years. Perhaps he is referring to "turning this thing around" by the year 2057 – the 100 year anniversary of the Lions last championship! I would be a 102 years old – can I make it?

Interesting article by Drew Sharpe in the Free Press on 12-17-05; "Revolt needs dose of Apathy." He reviews a problem between the players after week three of this season when the Lions got a very bad call that cost them the game at Tampa Bay. Supposedly, on the flight back home, Marcus Pollard, a new member of the team this year but a veteran of the NFL, was upset about the teams mood of "indifference." This apathy from the players bothered him greatly and he let them know about it. He stressed the need for professionalism that defines a successful organization. The players basically told Pollard to go to hell! That he "could take his attitude somewhere else." "It was obvious which direction this season was headed because apathy always trumps anger in sports." Outrage by the fans represents an emotional connection to the team – "if you're mad – they've still got you." "It's the uninterested that speaks loudest in the politics of sports management." Sharpe says, "if the players stopped caring, why shouldn't the fans?" He then goes on to describe the stages of grief as I did earlier in the book; denial, negotiation, anger and acceptance. He states correctly that we are in the anger stage. My point earlier in the book was that because of the addictive qualities of football fans, we may never get to acceptance. The advice is to "ignore the Lions. Walk away. Close your hearts as well as your wallets. It worked in Cincinnati."

◆◆◆

This is all correct in theory, but the problem lies in the power of the addiction. I propose the solution calls for all Lions fans to enter a 12 step program that we can call, "Lions Anonymous." If you don't face the addiction, recovery is impossible! There will be no way to progress to the stage of acceptance and stay away. The "drug" keeps calling you.

The fans in Cincinnati finally stayed away and helped the organization to change. Now, after 14 years out of the playoffs (the longest streak in the NFL), they will clinch their first trip since 1991 against the Lions tomorrow. "Lions fans think next time will be different. They will take another emotional shot to the gut, only to forgive once again." "Walking in protest doesn't suggest a change in attitude. The fans are mad. Only when they're prepared to silently walk away would the Lions actually listen to the screams." A brilliant article by Drew Sharp – one of the best written on the Lions this year.

An article by Bob Wojonowski in the Detroit News ('Its' going to be crazy') the same day said, "the Lions should consider this to be tough love from the fans, like one of those family interventions when someone refuses to admit a problem." "The NFL, with its parity-inducing salary cap, is set up for every team to get its turn. Almost every franchise has gotten a chance to sniff the top except the Lions." One player said, "It's not like the fans don't care." "Oh, they care. But today, as they march and chant and plead, they might ask themselves another question, a question that should scare the Lions even more. Why should they still care?" We know the answer to this one, don't we?

It was reported that the coach of the Vikings, Mike Tice, told his team to try to score early at Ford Field against the Lions, to make the fans turn on them. It worked! The Vikings first offensive play was an 80 yard touchdown pass and the fans were on their way.

Cincinnati 41-17 over the Lions. Not as much chaos and anger as was expected. A few chants of "Fire Millen." The 'angry fan march' was peaceful and had about 1000 fans attend. There were about 15% of the fans at the game wearing the Bengal's orange color; 5% of these were probably from Cincinnati. Dre' Bly said that when he saw Lions fans with the visiting team colors on, it decreased his energy for the game and upset him. There is always an excuse for Lions players. He also said after the game that not enough of the players take this serious enough. Now that is rather accurate based on this seasons' performance. The ex-great Lion Chris Spielman said that wearing the visiting team colors was going too far and was in poor taste from the fans.

This one was great from the start; the opening kickoff is fumbled by McQuarters without a hard hit. It was a terrible performance by the team. The only bright spot was the play of Harrington and Rogers, both of who will likely be gone after this year. Although word has it that Millen has not given up on Harrington. One of the local reporters who covers' the team, said that Mariucci virtually ignored Harrington the two and a half years he was here. He never tried to work with him to make him better; he was supposed to be good at developing young quarterbacks. That is remarkable news if it is true. Chad Johnson caught a touchdown pass and instead of celebrating as he usually did, looked confused and just handed the ball to the referee. "Maybe he figured the Lions weren't worth wasting the choreography." "Why waste your good stuff in practice." "The Lions handed this game to the Bengal's as if was government cheese." "The Lions starters were not introduced; instead, they raced out quickly, scattering to the sidelines like kids running from the cops."

The papers read, "no end in sight" and "home groan." Fire Millen bags were worn over heads. Posters of the three stooges, bozo the clown and Millen were seen. One fan in the stadium had a blue head band over his eyes saying "Lion – Vision"; blocking his sight. "Fans sat disconnected, occasionally booing, but unable to pump any energy, sarcastic or otherwise, into the place." The radio host who organized the march said, "its' about loving the Lions – we deserve better." A soldier wrote on his shirt, "I joined the marines to defend your right to watch this crap." Roy Williams said he felt the fans wanted the team to lose. A sign read, "ownership since 1963: one playoff win... Mr. Ford: who's the real problem?" "It's sad because it never gets answered." Mitch Albom wrote, "It wasn't the noise; it was the silence." "There goes another year." "Thank god it was the last home game; there's plenty of time to air out Ford Field before Super Bowl XL rolls around in February."

Michael Rosenberg wrote "It's not about bad football. That's nothing new. It's not even about historically bad football. It's about an organization that shows no signs of hope – and no stomach for the fundamental changes necessary to compete for a championship. They protest because they care. And they think the owner doesn't." This was very well stated.

◆◆◆

Things have quieted down quite a bit on the sports radio stations and the newspapers. No more jokes. Like what do the Lions and Billy Graham have in common? They can both get 70,000 people to say 'Jesus Christ' at the same time. There is the one describing a young boy who is in court before a judge. The boy has been abused and

77

beaten by most people in his family, so the judge asks him who he wants to live with. The boy says the 'Detroit Lions', because they can't beat anyone.

Harrington will start in New Orleans this weekend. Charles Rogers will be active for the game. This makes way too much sense! Who made this decision? Is Harrington being evaluated by Millen to see if he will be brought back next year? Or, is he playing in front of the Saints because there are reports that New Orleans is interested in Joey and have decided to let their QB Brooks go after the season is over? We will find out. Much of the current discussion is about the draft next spring. Most people feel we should pick an offensive lineman – there is a huge guy coming out of Virginia that is highly rated. This is all that is left for the woeful Lions fan – the draft in December.

What else can you say about the Lions' that hasn't already been said? Not much. I believe what happened in Detroit over the past month represented the first mass nervous breakdown by fans in sports history. We are in serious need of therapy, and lots of it! Am I the person for the job? I have a masters' degree in social work and significant experience with emotional and mental health problems. But am I ready to help fans cope with the grief, frustration and anger over this team? It's a major undertaking. Should I see people individually or in groups? Perhaps I should see three and four generations of families at the same time since this affliction affects 13 year olds up to 60 year olds.

An article in the Free Press reported that Jeff Garcia was so upset about his and the teams performance that he was "in tears, or close to tears." This is what the Lions can do to a veteran who appeared in three pro bowl games – bring them to tears! "What chance does a rookie have?" referring to Dan Orlovsky. Orlovsky is quoted in the article by Michael Rosenberg, saying "I want to be the quarterback of this team when they go to the Super Bowl." Isn't that a sweet thought? You can tell he is a rookie – give him a couple years for the realities of the Lions to set in.

◆◆◆

The article read, "They've suffered enough." It was about the two players on the Lions the longest; Jason Hanson, 13 years and Cory Schlesinger, 11 years. "You hope you can make it through it another week, after another loss, at the end of another losing season," said Hanson. "You talk to friends. You talk to family. It's not a good time to be a Lion." Schlesinger said "the fans are great, they love football, they love the Detroit Lions, that's why I love playing here." Even though he "did not care for the fans reaction," he realizes it is the players who need to look at themselves.

It would be very interesting to interview one of the players for the book. They are people trying to make a living for themselves and their families. I wonder how many players are really bothered by the losing, or accept that the Lions organization is not going to produce a winner and are grateful for a great job with a high income. I don't think a current player would be interested in being interviewed for this book since it is negative about the organization. Perhaps an ex-Lion who has no further relationship with the team?

◆◆◆

The Lions just beat the Saints 13-12 on a last second field goal by Hanson. It was very strange watching this. I was upset that they won the game. Why? Was it because I wanted that higher draft choice? Was it because it would be good material for my book? Or was it that I am sick of this organization and wish them only bad? This is a very strange feeling indeed.

I told my daughter that I had to drop her off at her grandparents at 12:30 instead of 2:00 because the Lions started at 1pm. NFL fans are so ingrained to be in front of their TV sets for the game, that Sundays are planed around the start time. I asked myself, based on how terrible this season has been, why do I care about getting home by 1pm? It's because we have done it all our lives - it's hard to not watch or ignore the magic of NFL football. I also needed to watch it in order to complete this book, and witness for myself the final moments of the 2005 season. I began writing this book one year ago after the Lions missed the extra point against the Vikings. So much has happened since.

The final few minutes of the Saints game was interesting. Roy Williams had dropped several balls during the game. The statistic shown was that Detroit and New Orleans led the NFL in dropped passes with 36 and 37 each. The Lions had about 12 penalties in this one, with five false starts. I was starting to say goodbye to Harrington as the game wound down. I was actually rooting for him at the start of the game. He led the team 75 yards down the field the first drive looking excellent, and then throws a horrible pass to Roy Williams in the end zone for an interception. He then gained only 55 yards during the second and third quarters. I felt that Harrington still might be very good in the NFL, but by the end of the game, I was again wanting him out of Detroit. This would be for Joey's sake and for the Lions. After Harrington fumbled the third down snap and looked ridiculous, it was fourth down and 17. I was waving goodbye to another game lost and goodbye to Harrington. He then throws a pass to Roy Williams which he makes a great catch on, out jumping the defender for a 40 or 50 yard gain to the Saints 35 yard line. It was a great catch. Usually I would be very excited. But I was pissed off that they made the play. Harrington hits Roy Williams for another completion; with no time outs, the field goal team runs out on the field. Why not spike the ball so the field goal team doesn't have to rush? It reminded me of the play earlier this year in college football when the Spartans did the same thing at the end of the half against Ohio State. They blocked the field goal and ran it back for a touchdown. The Lions executed the field goal perfectly (don't get to say that very often) and win the game as the clock runs out. Shawn Rogers TD on a fumble recovery was an amazing play, as he dragged three Saints 10 yards into the end zone; he is a special athlete and is going to the pro bowl. The Lions won this one without an offensive touchdown. We are playing at the Steelers the last game. Pittsburgh needs a win to make the playoffs. What do you think the result of this one will be?

The headlines read "Hanson unfazed by confusion." "There was a miscommunication on the sideline." Has this ever happened before? If that field goal would have failed, that's all we would have been talking about was why they didn't spike the ball after the first down. I heard the winning field goal called by Dan Miller on the radio; he sounded as though the Lions had just won the Super Bowl. "The kick is good; no time left on the clock, the Lions have won it - Merry Christmas!" It was sort of sad. We have to get excited about beating one of the worst three teams in the NFL, by the skin of our teeth.

❖❖❖

A song has come out about the Lions. I heard it on the radio this week. It sounded like it was making fun of the team of course. "It's the Lions I'll Buy" sung to the tune of Bye, Bye American Pie, from Lionbacker.com..

The Lions fight song is Gridiron Heroes. The lyrics are "Forward down the field, a charging team that will not yield. And when the blue and silver wave, stand and cheer the brave, Rah, Rah, Rah. Go hard win the game. With honor you will keep your fame. Down the field and gain, a Lion victory!

The song should read: Backward down the field, a doubting team that always yields. And when the blue and silver wave, close your eyes and pray, Rah, Rah, Rah. Go soft lose the game. With shame you will keep your name. Retreat the field and gain, another Lion loss! I am calling it Gridiron Zeroes.

❖❖❖

Here is an amazing statistic that says it all about the Lion offense this year. Through 15 games they are next to last in the NFL in TD passes with nine. Only the 49'ers have fewer with seven. You cannot win a lot of games with so few touchdown passes. The sports radio show today with Terry Foster talked about how the number of telephone calls into the show were 4:1 about the Lions vs. the Pistons. We have the 5-10 Lions vs. the 22-3 Pistons; a team that has appeared in five NBA Finals in 17 years and has won three of the five. The Pistons are a team that lost both Finals in game seven in dramatic fashion. They are a team that is off to the second greatest start of an NBA season in the history of the league. When I called into the show, my point was that the fans are not so much addicted to the Lions as they are to the NFL game. The Lions are all we have.

Listening to sports radio today it is clear the "Lions illness" is starting to affect the hosts. Tony Ortiz and Terry Foster almost get into a fight over the Lions. Terry was upset that Tony said that the media has fueled the fire regarding the expectations for the Lions this year. Terry felt it was the Lions that fueled that fire and reporters only passed that on to fans. When I called in to comment about the rift, the screener told me they were only taking calls on the Pistons. The Lions debate went on another hour.

One of the funny aspects of this show on December 27th, 2005 was when Terry Foster said that the Super Bowl for Lions fans is draft day in April. "The Lions could draft a Saint Bernard and they could sell it to their fans. The dog is really fast and will put us over the top"! Or they could draft a smurf or the pepsi machine, and they would find a way to spin it to the fans. Are we that stupid? I think we are.

The picture in the Free Press of Garcia and Harrington with backs to each other, looking depressed says it all.

"Worst season ever?" The article by Steve Schrader says "We learned long ago not to ask, can it get any worse than this? Because that's like daring the Lions to show it can. Sure they have had worse records, but with them imploding and the fans revolting, there are reasons to call 2005 their worst season ever." The article ends by saying "but at least they're (fans) still coming to the games."

❖❖❖

The paper of 12-29-05 reads "Steely determination awaits lowly Lions." "The article by Nicholas Cotsonika says "as Dick Jauron spoke, thunder rolled and rain beat down on the roof of the Lions indoor practice facility. The team headquarters, intended to be open and airy, was dim and gray. It set the appropriate mood. This has been a stormy, gloomy season for the Lions, and it won't end until they weather one more game, Sunday at Pittsburgh." "The Lions continue to talk about playing for pride, being professional, auditioning for their futures, that sort of thing. None seem motivated to reach six victories." What a surprise that none of the players this reporter talked to "seem motivated." They haven't seemed motivated all year. Is it because they aren't being paid enough?

❖❖❖

I was talking to my good friend Chuck recently about football and the Lions. Chuck played college football in division three as a half back and coached high school football for 20 years, 10 as an assistant and 10 as a head coach. He felt the key to turning the Lions around was changing the attitude in the organization and with the fan base, that these are "the same old Lions." He feels that starts with the owner and filters down. He believes the importance of the head coach is over rated. He doesn't believe this attitude can change as long as W.C. Ford owns the team. He talked about owners like Jerry Jones, Al Davis, Kraft and others that have been successful in breeding a successful, positive attitude. When Chuck goes to a Lions game, it is for the "event." "It's about being with friends or family, going to Greek town or the casinos, and watching a little bit of the game". When he watches football at any level, he analyzes blocking schemes and formations to figure out what the coach is trying to do. He does this when he knows the team is very good. He does not do this when watching the Lions – it's "entertainment only."

Chuck feels most Lions fans don't really know the game of football. They got free tickets or are coming for a company function. When there are only 16 games, each game is magnified compared to other sports that play so many more. Why are the Lions so talked about? Chuck asked 'why are soap operas so popular." People love to see what is going to go wrong next, its human nature. He feels the NFL game is so different; it's not just the skill or talent level – it's about the drive to be the best. The pride one has in being the best. Some pros get complacent; I get my money whether we are 2-14 or 14-2. The adrenaline rush that is critical may not be there for some players. NFL football is the most emotional game of any played. You get to focus on one team for a week; grown men crying after tough losses.

Although you have to have talent to win, you can "hide" less talented guys through your schemes. The chemistry that is critical takes years to develop in an organization. Sixty or more people working towards a common goal can be a very powerful experience for all involved. You have to have emotional bonds to each other. We talked about how close the Pistons are as teammates. A reporter last year during the Finals couldn't believe that 11 of the players went out to dinner one night with each other. Chuck also talked about football being a game of "sudden changes." You plan for a game and then injuries, turnovers and strange plays can change those plans in an instant. It is a game of constant thinking on your feet. When discussing half time adjustments, Chuck felt it was the players informing the coaches of what was happening that was the key. Chuck had a memorable season as the head coach of the Dearborn Pioneers in 1995. His team ended up 10-0; undefeated and un-scored upon – 10 straight shutouts! It was only the second time in high school history that has happened. ESPN ran a story on the team that year. Unfortunately, the team lost to the third ranked team in the state of Michigan and did not make it to the championship game.

❖❖❖

The sports talk shows are dying down a bit about the Lions. I think we are preparing for the relief that comes from having seven months away from the frustrations and disappointment of yet another lost season. A few comments included predictions of a 6-10 record next year and the hiring of the Lions first black head coach. There was some controversy over comments by Damion Woody which were reported; he said that if he knew about the problems in the Lions organization, he would have never come to Detroit. That kind of remark is just what the team needs in trying to bring other quality free agents here. He took a very high salary from Detroit and callers were questioning if he played well enough to earn it and say things like that. Once again, finger pointing, a lack of loyalty and chaos. A lot of the player comments the past month as the wheels fell off, were clear as to the problems of attitude, chemistry and professionalism that have existed on the Lions for many years. Or has it been just a simple fact of not enough talent? I don't know anymore; I think I'm overloaded on this team and am looking forward to the break from the daily analysis.

This 'Lion illness' can be so hard to figure out. I was telling my buddy the other day about my good friend thinking of giving up his two tickets on the 25 yard line, 17th row - very close to the field. After telling everyone I know that I was not renewing my terrible upper deck seats next year, my first reaction to my friend was "no!, me and Larry will take them." What is it about this illness that gets such a grip on you? Is it that it is the only affordable season ticket of the four major sports due to how few games are played? Is it the NFL magic that has waiting lists of 5-10 years in some cities? I will figure it out someday.

❖❖❖

Dec. 31, 2005 – we say goodbye to another year. It was another year of frustration for the Lions and their fans. The Free Press reads "Lions in Limbo – Who will return?" "Final Curtain?" "Endgame for Joey, Jauron and Rogers?" Drew Sharp writes that Harrington "needs a fresh start." "If that means forcing his way out of town, leaving the Lions with the suicidal task of finding both a number one and two quarterback in the off season through free agency or trades, then so be it. Turn the screws to 'em." "If a player has the chance to orchestrate his exit out of this insane asylum, why wouldn't he?" "Joey has always conducted himself cordially and professionally." I agree, get out while you can Joey!

The Lions record at Pittsburgh is 0-5-1 since their last victory on Nov. 13, 1955. Let's see, I was two and a half weeks old when that last win took place at Pittsburgh! "When you've waited a half century, what's a little more?" I'm predicting a 31-3 halftime score. And the final score of 44-10.

What do I know? The Steelers lead 21-14 at half. Harrington looks fantastic throwing two TD passes and a QB rating of 146! But of course the Lions are the Lions, and Eddie Drummond fumbles a punt leading to the go ahead touchdown. Special teams allow an 81 yard TD on a punt return, and another return for 63 yards that Hansen saves. A fumble late in the half by the Lions almost leads to another score, but Pittsburgh throws an interception on the last play. It is the best the offense has looked all year, against the third ranked defense in the NFL. Jimmy Johnson says the Lions should keep Matt Millen and Dick Jauron for next year. Howie Long says the Lions are like a bad stock; up and down, up and down. I don't recall much up, do you? Terry Bradshaw makes hand motions like a fish flopping back and forth. We are so proud of our team!

I am listening to the start of the second half while I am working on the book. No need to see it – I can hear the predictable TD drive quickly down the field by the Steelers; 28-14 – it will get worse. Bettis gets his third TD of the day in his final home appearance. The Lions come back on Harrington's third TD pass of the day to Roy Williams. This is after Williams dropped an easy 20 yard pass earlier in the drive. Harrington and the offense looks the best it has all season. The amazing statistic shown about Bill Cower and the Steelers; they are 99-1-1 when leading a game by 11 points or more.

Pittsburgh scores again; 35-21 as the third quarter comes to an end. 15 minutes left of our Lions this year. Thank god! It's been a long, painful year for us fans. I'm sure it has been similar for the players, but at least they get paid to deal with this. Detroit gets an interception with seven minutes left. During the drive, a 20 yard pick up by Roy Williams is taken away because Kevin Jones is called for illegal procedure. Key mistakes at the worst times are a Lions trademark. Harrington is 2-9 since being on fire. Pittsburgh has had only two head coaches since 1969 – amazing!

Chapter 10

Thank God the 2005 season is over!

Thank God the season is over. Final score Steelers 35-21. I thought it would have been much worse. You have to give the players and Jauron credit for playing hard and preparing for this one. I guess they do have professional pride as athletes. Jauron told the team to be prepared for the Steelers to try to 'crush' them because of the playoff implications of the game. This game showed that the talent on the team is not as bad as their record. As the Free Press stated on 1-2-05, "the Lions are suffocated by a losing mentality." The headlines read, "Steelers drop curtain on Lions." "Lost! Can lowly Lions be rescued?"

Mike O'Hara wrote in his column "the Lions have a national image of a franchise in disarray, with players who lack talent or underachieve – or both. We took a beating in the public eye, said Woody. It's a perception of you. You are guilty by association. You mention you play for the Detroit Lions - you're looked at like a villain. It's not fair. There are a lot of guys here who get it." O'Hara points out the five keys to fixing this organization; 1) Hire the right coach, 2) Settle on a quarterback and support him, 3) Fix the offense, 4) Change attitudes and 5) Leadership.

Now what? No more waiting for Sunday at 1p.m. anymore. I will watch the playoffs and the Super Bowl as a fan of the NFL, but it's nothing compared to watching your team in the post season. The healing can now begin for all of us once again. It will take two to four weeks for some of the bitterness to go away. Talk radio will continue its daily obsession with the Lions with talk of the new coach, the draft, the players coming back and management. It won't die down until after the Super Bowl. From February through April is when the majority of healing takes place. We are sucked back in for the draft. Then as August approaches with the first pre-season game, we will once again believe our Lions will make it this year. The seasons changing are like a re-birth of life and hope. From now until the next NFL season, the fans of Detroit are lucky enough to have the Red Wings and the Pistons. They will get us through the long, cold winter.

◆◆◆

I will finish this book soon. I love this football team we call the Detroit Lions. I love the city of Detroit. It's part of who I am as a person. I will continue to recover my mental health, but my addiction is a life long problem. A relapse can occur at any time. I know I am getting healthier because I am committed to following through on giving up my season tickets.

The Free press reviews the coaching candidates. Carthon from Cleveland, Lewis of the Giants, Grimm of the Steelers, Saunders of the Chiefs, Schwartz of the Titans and Singletary of the 49'ers. Mike O'hara feels Carthon would be the best choice because he comes from the "Bill Parsells training ground. Carthon has an intense, no-excuses work ethic that matches the personality of Lions president Matt Millen." "Whoever Millen hires, the Powder Puff Spa is closed. Get ready to work, Lions."

The radio talk shows on the day after the season ended for Detroit is 100% Lions talk. Spindler and Caputo spent two straight hours talking about the coaches available after several more were fired, interviewing Jeff Garcia and taking calls from fans. Little talk about the bowls, the college national championship in two days, or the 24-4 Pistons. This is what the 'disease' can do to you.

The radio stations reported that the win at New Orleans giving them five for the season cost them the number two pick overall. We could have had Matt Leinart from USC! We could have had the top offensive lineman from Virginia Tech. We now will pick ninth. Even when they win, the Lions get it wrong. Shawn Merriman from San Diego, a defensive end is going to the Pro Bowl. He was available when Detroit picked Mike Williams at number 10. It looks like another bad choice, doesn't it?

◆◆◆

1-3-06, the headlines read "Now, We Wait." "Season of turning points – all downward." Damion Woody recalled the 21-20 loss to Carolina as a key game. "When your defense scores two touchdowns, causes four turnovers and you still lose, that's bad. That's real bad. We couldn't do anything on offense. That might have been the worse offense I've ever seen." There was another interesting statement from Joey Harrington. "I would go somewhere to be valued. If a head coach said to me, you know what? We think you're the best number two quarterback in this league, and we value you as that; that may be good enough for me." These articles were from Nicholas Cotsonika. That is a pretty amazing statement from Harrington. Most guys want the starting quarterback job only. Especially at 27 years old! I guess the statement brings in the human factor that people need to be valued and wanted. He has felt very little of that in Detroit. I believe him when he says it will not be about money. Harrington has made almost $30 million in Detroit in four years. He is set for life with money. The article by Drew Sharp said that Millen should come out from hiding and explain how he will go about his search for a head coach. "Silence becomes arrogance, and Millen has remained silent since he fired Mariucci."

Millen said recently that "the new coach's challenge would be to
change the team's attitude. The one thing that doesn't exist right now
for whatever reason is confidence and a belief, and those things can
take talent and push it to a whole other level. You've seen it happen,
I've seen it happen. We're watching it happen right now in the league
in the playoffs. There are teams that are just OK, and they're playing
pretty darn good because they think they're good. It makes a big
difference."

The headlines on 1-4-06 read "Millen: I share your pain." Haven't we
heard that before from a guy in the White House? "Millen's plan C."
The articles by Nicholas Cotsonika said "I didn't blame those people
one bit. I was more ticked off than they were." Millen was referring
to the anger by the fans. Millen "breaks his silence and vows never
to quit." Millen said "To be honest with you, this hurt this year. It
really, really bothered me." I sure hope it bothered him! "I didn't
sleep very well; my hair turned white. This was the worst thing I ever
went through." "My blood pressure went through the roof." "Millen,
47, didn't want to discuss whether he had offered to step down or
if team owner William Clay Ford had given him a private vote of
confidence. But clearly both have happened." Millen said, "I mean
this sincerely: I wouldn't trade positions with any GM in the league.
And you want to know why? Because I believe what we have here is
going to work. I believe that 100%, and I believe the people in this
building believe that." "Maybe no one else believes in us. Maybe
they don't. They don't have to. Only we have to believe it." Wow,
that is a rather confident thing to say. I have to give it to Millen; he
has guts and he must be pretty tough to have survived this. Are you
sure you don't want to trade places with the GM at New England?

The fan reaction to Millen's interview was amazing! The anger just
won't go away. They will not give Millen a break. Maybe I'm just
a sap, but his comments significantly increased my respect for him,
and gave me some hope that this could turn around. Millen has been
learning on the job, and I believe the learning curve may be turning.
Fan comments on 1-5-06 from the Free Press included; "tell Millen
to stop blowing smoke and get out of town. His only pain would be

losing all that money; I was more ticked off than you were! Uh...no you weren't, Matt. Believe me, no you weren't; Millen could find a way to destroy the Colts; that was a heartwarming story about Mr. Millen. The only difference in our pain is $3 million and free beer instead of one that costs $7. He is the biggest con man to come to town since Professor Harold Hill in Music Man; Millen has done everything to convince me he's not the man to fix the Lions. He took over a 9-7 team and gave us the worst record in the NFL. Thanks to the Fords, we have another five years of his mess; give Matt another year. He promised not to draft anymore wide receivers in the first round. In fact, he is focusing on a quality long snapper from Rhode Island State to draft with the Lions first pick. Matt feels that if you are going to rebuild a team you must rebuild around the long snapper. That eliminates any further quarterback controversy; Millen hired Marty (the bar is high) Mornhinwig, a real clown. He followed with Steve (two yards, two yards, two yards, punt) Mariucci. Matt's track record indicates he will pick the most incompetent man for the job; wow, what a heart-wrenching story about a man with such compassion and drive. This leader has been definitely misunderstood by the public. He speaks of his new grey hair and the pain he has had to endure this year. Well, you should see my grey hair. I'm a season-ticket holder and he is raking in the money. Fans have had to endure this pain since 1957; Millen says he wants the right guy with the right qualities for the Lions. What? Do fans care if the Lions fit Detroit? Matt, the fans care about WINNING and that's it! If that's his plan, then what he's really saying is that he has no idea, none, on what to do."

❖❖❖

Writing this book has taught me several things. One, that I know nothing about the NFL or football in general, other than my opinion as a fan. Fans love to feel like they know more than the players, coaches and administrators. It's all an ego thing. For instance, Rob Parker of the Detroit News wrote a column on 1-5-06 where he ripped Millen apart. It was very sarcastic and demeaning to Millen and the Lions. "Hey, Millen, here's some advice, and its free of charge.

Now it's time for Millen to listen and take notes. It couldn't hurt to take some advice from a columnist who knows a little something about football. If Millen were in school, this would be considered cheating. After all, this column has given him all the answers to his most important test yet. Good luck, Millen. You'll need it." Parker's major advice was to hire Maurice Carthon as the new head coach and bring in Aaron Brooks as the quarterback. What brilliant advice! I wonder why Parker hasn't been hired as a GM in the NFL? He's probably interviewing as I speak.

What an ego this guy has! It is one of the most arrogant sports articles I have ever seen, and I think the author looks like a fool. I hate to tell Mr. Parker this, but he doesn't really know much more than any other fan of the Lions. I can see why NFL teams get sick of the fans and the media.

Saturday 1-7-06, there is nothing written in the Free Press about the Lions. It is the first time this has happened probably since May of 2005. Things are starting to die down. It's time to move on and start the healing process. When they select the new coach, things will start up again. Until then, heal Lions fans, heal!

◆◆◆

We are down to the final eight teams who have a chance to win Super Bowl 40 in Detroit in less than a month. Here are the eight with previous Super Bowl appearances and wins: Indianapolis (2/1), New England (5/3), Pittsburgh (5/4), Denver (6/2), Carolina (1/0), Washington (5/3), Chicago (1/1) and Seattle (0/0). Only Seattle has never appeared in the big game, but their coach, Mike Holmgren has won super bowls with the Packers. The coaches are Dungy, Belichick, Cower, Shanahan, Fox, Gibbs, Smith and Holmgren; a rather solid group of coaches. four of the eight have Super Bowl rings. What is their secret? Why won't they share it with the Lions?

I was listening to sports radio about a discussion on the Lions coaching search. Tom Kowalski said that the Lions are being very quiet about who is interviewing. They don't want the other NFL teams to find out and 'jump on the band wagon" and steal those coaches away. I thought how funny that sounded. You would think that other teams would stay away from anyone the Lions would be interested in based on their track record of hiring coaches.

The Sports Inferno radio talk show discussed the Lions coaching search. Word around the league was that Detroit was once again "the joke of the NFL" because they have targeted Russ Grimm as the next coach. Instead of seriously considering the coaches as they interview, word is they are token interviews to give the impression that they are doing it the right way. Millen supposedly wants Grimm. One of his buddies he played with. Grimm is a tough guy who would instill discipline and motivation, but word is that when he did not get the job at Chicago or Cleveland last year, it was because of some short comings. It has been reported that he did not interview well; comes to interviews in very casual dress. He wore a sweat suit to the final interview for the Chicago Bears coach last year, which he lost to Lovie Smith. Also, that he is not a very organized person. If this is true, there are serious questions about his professionalism and his administrative abilities. I'm guessing it might be important for a head coach in the NFL to have organizational skills. The other concern is that the Lions are the only team looking for a head coach that had a face to face interview with Grimm. The Packers had a telephone interview scheduled with him, but cancelled when they selected a different guy. And the Saints have had a telephone interview with him. Does that concern any one else? I am feeling that they should get Hasslett before the Bills sign him. But what do I know? The Lions have interviewed nine candidates by reports as of 1-13-06. We will see who the Lions select as their next leader. God help them!

We are down to the last four teams. The Steelers will play at Denver and the Panthers at Seattle. There was an amazing end to the Steelers/Colts game. Pittsburgh deserved to win the game though, due to two very bad calls by the refs. The Bettis fumble was shocking, and almost cost the Steelers the game. We root for Bettis since he is a

Detroit native. It would be great if he could play his last game in Detroit for the title. I felt bad for Payton Manning and Tony Dungy. The death of Dungy's son affected the entire team. But Pittsburgh and the Broncos were very smart defensively; they used many blitzes on Manning and Brady to change their flow. I never understood why the Lions have given opposing QB's all day to throw. But, again, I am a fan – what do I know? I predict the Super Bowl will be Seattle against Denver. Since the Steelers are playing this week, Detroit cannot offer Grimm the head coaching job. I hope they give it to Hasslett.

The Lions are talking to Rod Marinelli today – a second interview for the defensive line coach of the Tampa Bay Bucs. He is in his late 50's, but has never been a head coach or a coordinator. Some people think he may be interviewing for a defensive coordinator position under Grimm. There is no way he could be the head coach, since his last name starts with an 'M'. Please, no more 'M's!

The word is that Jim Haslett will be named the Lions new coach by the end of this week. I feel it is a better choice than Russ Grimm of the Steelers. Haslett has been a head coach for five years and before that was a defensive coordinator at Pittsburgh under Cowar. I would rather take my chances on an experienced guy vs. a guy who will learn on the job. We have seen the results from that strategy. Haslett was 10-6 with the Saints in 2000 but has been at .500 since except for last year with the Katrina mess. He was a linebacker for the Bills and has that tough guy look of a head coach. Some guy called in a sports radio show and said that if Haslett was hired as the next coach, he would slice his wrists! I guess he sees it different than I do. The truth is that no one knows who will be a great head coach. Only time will tell.

❖❖❖

1-18-06; we've got our man – Rod Marinelli, the defensive line coach and assistant head coach of the Tampa bay Bucs. Another M & M combination; our fourth one! First it was Millen and Moeller, then

Millen and Mornhinwig, then Millen and Mariucci and now Millen and Marinelli. What are the odds of four straight coaches having a last name starting with 'M'?

The headlines read, "Next... Lions hire who?" and "M & M again! The media will not stop the insults. Drew Sharpe wrote that he doesn't trust the hire, because it was made by "people who don't know what their doing." I don't think today is the day to attack the Lions. I do believe they went about the search the right way and are trying their best to get this right. As I have said, fans and media don't really know what they are talking about for the most part. It is probably harder than it looks to run a professional sports organization. Millen was interviewed on the radio after announcing Marinelli as the new coach. He was obviously in a good mood, and told a funny story. After arriving home from New Orleans with their 13-12 win at 1 a.m., he walked in his house on Christmas Eve and saw a sign on top of the Christmas tree. It said "Fire Millen." I guess his wife has a pretty good sense of humor. It has only been a few weeks since the end of the Lions' season, and you can tell that my anger is going away. I am starting to feel my mental health returning. Defending the Lions; aren't you impressed?

It will be very interesting to see who he brings in as his coordinators, what type of offense he decides to run and what he does about the quarterback situation. There is no question that our defense will be significantly improved. The talk shows should be non-stop about the Lions through the Super Bowl as Marinelli puts his staff together. Is there any chance I could be the team social worker?

I have to say that everything being said about this man is very impressive. I actually think that Millen may have gotten it right this time. He looks like a very tough minded guy who will supply organization and energy onto the team. With his cap on, he reminds me of Tom Landry from the Cowboys years ago. The sports reporter from Tampa said that he feels Detroit got the best coach of all the ones hired over these past few weeks. One of the Tampa Bay players called Marinelli the "best coach he has ever played for." Does Marinelli realize just what he has gotten into? It usually means the end of your career is close when you join the Lions! Good luck Rod, you will need it.

The headlines about Marinelli continue for a few days. "This Lion Roars!" For the most part fans feel he was a good choice, but there remains significant skepticism. There will be more Lions discussion as he puts together his staff. Today, on the two major talk radio stations, they were talking about the Tigers and baseball. The heat is finally off the Lions.

The Steelers will play the Seahawks in Super Bowl 40 in two weeks here in Detroit. These are two great teams and it is hard to pick a winner. I am leaning towards the Steelers in a close one. I am happy for the Seattle fans – they can now be taken off the list of teams that have never been to the Super Bowl. Are the Lions still on that list?

I just saw that Dick Jauron will be named the new head coach of the Buffalo Bills today. This has to be the first time a coach from the Lions has gone onto a head coaching job somewhere else in the NFL. I can only think of Don Shula going as an assistant with Detroit to the Miami Dolphins as their head coach in the 1960's. Usually, when you leave the Lions, your career in the NFL is over. I can see it now – the Bills go 12-4 next year and Jauron takes them to the Super Bowl, while Marinelli sucks and the Lions are 6-10 again. That might qualify for an "I Don't Believe It."

There is very little talk about the Lions at this point. The focus is clearly on Super Bowl XL. There will be more focus on the Lions once Marinelli names his staff and we get closer to draft day in April. The fans in Seattle went crazy when they earned their first trip to the big game. That is how I envision Lions fans if we ever get a chance at that moment. I am much more positive these days, now that there are no games to play. I do believe I will see Detroit in the big game if I can make it until 90 years old. That gives them 40 seasons to get it right!

Henderson from the Jets has been named the defensive coordinator for Detroit. He worked under Herm Edwards who is very well respected. The receivers' coach of the Bengal's is said to be the front runner for the offensive coordinator position. It is very strange not hearing much about the Lions after a daily barrage for three months. I bet the players are enjoying their break - it couldn't have been much fun this past season, or these past five seasons! I heard that a reporter came out with a list of the top 10 worst executives in professional sports. Guess where Millen ended up? Right, at number one!

❖❖❖

I am using 'Lions logic' to predict the winner of Super Bowl XL. The Lions played the Steelers tough the last day of the season. It was their best performance against a quality team this year. Because the Steelers struggled against Detroit, I am picking the Seahawks to win the big one. I will be rooting for Bettis and the Steelers, but Lions logic is full proof!

January 30, 2006 – the radio talk shows are discussing the possible hire of Mike Martz as the Lions offensive coordinator. Mike Valenti of WXYT 1270 who is an outstanding radio host was on the air. He also has a big ego and thinks he knows enough to run the Lions as their president. Everything out of his mouth about the Lions is negative. He has an amazing sense of humor and way with words. Today he said that the Lions were "idiots" and you can't trust any decision they make. He said the "Lions make the Arizona Cardinals seem like the Vince Lombardi led Green Bay Packers." He also said that Detroit had "an abortion of an offensive line." He is hoping the Lions pick the wide receivers coach from the Bengal's as the next offensive coordinator.

There are six days left until the Super Bowl. My numbers in my pool are terrible. I have Seattle two and Pittsburgh nine. Someone told me that the final score a few years ago was 32-29. I need a repeat. My buddy Al who is working the Super Bowl as the radio engineer told me he might let me assist him for the Maxim party on Saturday night.

I hear it is one of the biggest parties at the Super Bowl. Wouldn't that be amazing!

◆◆◆

One month after the Lions' season ended, I can think more clearly about what this has all been about. I believe that all the passion, intensity, anger over the Lions' failures represents our need for hope. Hope for the future. There has to be something to look forward to during the boredom of everyday life. The reason Lions fans have hope as August rolls around, is because we need to believe in something; need to look forward to something. Even though, the reality of the past decades tells us that there is little chance of success, we believe this year can be different. Like my son Jason would tell me when he was a little boy, "you never know Dad." Everyone needs hope in life. When we say there is a chance this year, it has nothing to do with reality. It has to do with the human spirit that holds onto hope even when reality tells us otherwise.

The word is that Mike Martz will be named the Lions offensive coordinator today. He will get a one year contract worth two million dollars. If this is true, the Lions have themselves their best coaching staff in their history. It will be Marinelli, Henderson and Martz. I think Millen has learned from his mistakes. The fans have got to be excited about this. All the talk will die down after the Super Bowl as we move towards the Red Wing playoffs in April and the Pistons playoffs in May. It will get hot again a few weeks before the NFL draft in April. Could this coaching staff be the turn around that the Lions so desperately need?

◆◆◆

The headlines read "XL-ENT." The Steelers win 21-10 over the Seahawks. I thought it was a boring game, but Pittsburgh won because of three big plays. Roethlesberger had a QB rating of 22 - the lowest ever for a winning quarterback. He did hit a few big passes and ran very effectively. He was also the youngest QB to ever win the big game. Bettis gets the big win in his home town and announces his retirement after the game. What a way to go out! Pittsburgh wins their fifth Super Bowl, tying them with the 49'ers and Dallas with the most wins. The NFL season is over. We will miss football until August. Detroit did a great job hosting the Super Bowl, and improved its image greatly. I went to the Maxim party - what an amazing experience talking to athletes and Hollywood stars.

Jimmy Kimmel did his show live from Detroit and wrote a goodbye letter to the people on a full page ad in the Detroit Free Press. "To my new friends in Detroit, you did not have to be so friendly, you did not have to welcome us with open arms, you did not have to put extra chili on our Coney dogs, but you did. This is a great city, full of great people and no matter what anyone ever says; you have nothing to be ashamed of (except maybe the Lions). On behalf of my co-workers, my family, and ABC, thanks you for being so nice. You made us feel like one of your own and we won't ever forget it. I hope to come back soon. Your pals, Jimmy Kimmel and the crew of Jimmy Kimmel live." This was a very nice note about our city. The pride one has in the town you grew up in or live in as an adult. It's about who you are. Loving our football team is also about loving our city and our neighbors.

Of course, Kimmel couldn't just keep it genuine - he had to make the comment about the Lions. He is a comedian, so we shouldn't be surprised. That is the national perception; that our football team sucks. Until we change and become a winning organization, we will be the butt of jokes.

Another national writer for ESPN.com, David Fleming, wrote "I'm not trying to pretend that Detroit is perfect. It's not. Far from it. Pollution. Poverty. Education. Racial tentions. Unemployment. The Lions." He ends his article saying, "what I'm trying to say is, you're Detroit, damn it, home of Joe Louis, Tommy Hearns, Gordie Howe, Kid Rock, WRIF and the toughest, most loyal fans in the NFL." We probably are the toughest NFL fans in the country; us, Cleveland, Arizona and New Orleans. Fans from these cities better be tough to survive the many years of frustration our teams have given us.

❖❖❖

The Lions signed Mike Martz to a three year contract as their offensive coordinator. The three new coaches, Marinelli, Martz and Henderson sound like a solid group of leaders. There is definitely reason for hope and optimism, as there is every year. The way I will approach it next year as a fan will be to watch the Lions the first 10 games before I make any judgments or let myself become too attached to the team. They are going to have to show me things are different. I will not invest any money in the team at this point. The season tickets are gone. My hope is they can win six or seven of the first 10 games and have a shot at the playoffs. If so, the final six games could be very interesting starting around Thanksgiving when we play the Miami Dolphins. Good luck gentleman, you may need it. Most important, good luck to the players – it looks like things may be a little different around here regardless of the record.

The Harrington era is officially over. The Lions signed Kitna and McCowen to compete for the starting position. They will either trade him or cut him from the team. It was reported that there were some problems during a recent quarterback mini-camp with Harrington and the new coaching staff. They either didn't like his attitude and effort, or Joey told Millen that he changed his mind and didn't want to remain a Lion. We may never know. This may be best for both the Lions and Harrington, but it is clearly a blow to have to walk away from the third overall pick in the draft four years ago. In an article by Mitch Albom of the Detroit Free Press on May 15, 2006, Joey described the moment he knew he and Mariucci were in trouble. He came into Mariucci's office and told him that they needed to open up the offense. Mariucci walked over to a sink, began brushing his teeth, and told Harrington he had interviews to conduct and to come back later if he wanted to discuss it. This tells you a great deal about the coach and problems on the team. It looks like Joey may end up with the Dolphins – see you on Thanksgiving!

It's April 29, 2006 – Super Bowl day for Lions fans! It's the NFL draft. During a mock draft this week, Drew Sharpe of the Free Press picked Matt Leinart in the ninth position. Before he made the pick, he said that these college players are nice kids and have never done anything wrong, but they are about to hear the six dreaded words no college player wants to hear; "you are now a Detroit Lion." I thought this was hilarious.

Michael Rosenberg of the Free Press wrote that the Lions were looking for character players. That might leave Vince Young out since he "wore jeans to the white house and supposedly took one look at the Wonderlic Test and spent the next 30 minutes licking it." "If Vince Young dropped to the ninth pick and the Lions pass on him, Young would inevitably develop into a combination of Michael Vick, Johnny Unitas and Thomas Edison. This is precisely the kind of thing that happens to the Lions."

We select Ernie Sims out of Florida State with the ninth pick in the first round. He is an outside linebacker who is punishing towards opponents'. The only problem he presents is that he hits people so hard that he has had five concussions in his college career. The Lions said they have had him checked out medically, and doctors feel he will be fine. I can see it now; he is a great player for one or two seasons but has to retire because of head trauma. He sounds like a great young man who might provide emotion and leadership to the defense.

We selected a safety and a running back in the second and third rounds. We did get two offensive linemen in the late rounds which may be a good move. The debate was that the Lions had both Matt Leinart and Jay Cutler available at their first pick, but went for defensive help. I agreed with the decision, but knowing the Lions luck or lack of it, you just know that one of them will become a star quarterback in the NFL.

Stop the presses! May 5, 2006 – one or more of the Lions players complained to the union that Marinelli had contact drills in practice which violated the players' agreement. "I Don't Believe It!"
You have to be kidding me; the player(s) told their mommies that the coach was being mean to them. "He was making us hit each other mommy; didn't you tell us never to do that? We miss our old coach – Coach Mariucci was nice; we had more fun with him. Maybe the union can get us back our nice coach." I'm joking guys – don't come after me now. I'm old and I break easily! A report on May 17, 2006 identified three players who made the complaint; Shawn Rogers, James Hall and Marcus Bell.

When I was telling my girlfriends' sister about this, her three month old son was on her lap. Her baby had been fine for the hour I saw him, but he began crying when he heard me say the word 'Lions'. The boys name is Vance Spielman, no relationship to Chris. Was this a coincidence or not? I think poor little Vance can sense his NFL team is probably going to bring tears to his eyes many more times as he grows up. I think Chris Spielman would have been appalled by a player complaining about a hard practice.

This tells you a great deal about the previous head coach, the new coach and the players. I guess you might consider the player who made the report 'soft'. I can see anyone on the Steelers, Patriots, or Cowboys making this type of complaint. Their coaches would pull them by their ears and smash their heads into a wall. The team losses two days of practice time as a penalty. The players get two days off that are paid. Marinelli must be fuming! I'm guessing that the player or players may not have a very good year with their coaches. If they are fringe players, they may be done in Detroit very soon. I would think the rest of the team is rather embarrassed by this. The Lions are already the laughing stock of the NFL; can you imagine the new jokes coming out of this incident?

A radio ad on May 23, 2006, trying to sell club level seats at Ford Field for the Lions this year, said "for the best sports experience in Detroit." A few weeks ago, the Lions came out with a statement in the newspaper that they "provide one of the best game day experiences in the NFL at Ford Field", and choose not to have cheerleaders for the team. An ex-cheerleader said that they should probably have a cheer squad so "at least someone would be cheering for them." It's amazing the Lions can even say these things publicly; I guess they might be true if winning football games is not important.

Chapter 11

Where do we go from here?

As I finish this book, this labor of love, I have decided to end on a positive note. I was listening to sports talk radio and heard Chris Spielman talk about the recent Super Bowl. He said that he cannot go to any Super Bowls because it kills him that he never played in one. His wife and kids went to one a few years ago, and he stayed at home. He also talked about how he still "obsesses" about what he could have done differently in the 1991 NFC championship game where the Lions got blown out by the Redskins. It hit me just what football meant to this man.

The show concluded by saying that if Lions fans could pick two of their players to play in a Super Bowl it would be Barry Sanders and Chris Spielman.

To know the quality of this man you need look no further than Spielman as a husband. He took a year off from his NFL career when he was with Cleveland, to care for his wife who was being treated for breast cancer. We sometimes forget that players are human beings, with problems like all of us. Chris Speilman is one of the most inspiring athletes I have followed as a Detroit sports fan. He is up there with Gordie Howe, Steve Yzerman, Al Kaline, Barry Sanders, and Isiah Thomas. Although Chris never got his NFL championship, he always had the heart of a champion.

My friend Al who has worked the Lions games for years told me a great story about Spielman recently. When he came into the Silver dome Sunday mornings, Spielman would be there watching film at 9:30 a.m. This may not be that unusual, except that it was widely known that he usually watched film on his opponent all of Saturday night falling asleep in the film room. When I heard this story, everything about why I wrote this book became clear. It's about passion for players and fans. It's about hard work and keeping the faith. It's about loving your team and your city.

The Detroit Lions hold a very special place in the hearts and minds of the fans and the city. We have been lucky enough to enjoy championships with six other teams; three pro and three college. But there is nothing like NFL football. We will continue to dream and hope that our Lions get this right someday. Until then we will endure the tough seasons and torturous loses. Maybe, just maybe someday we can watch our team in the big game. Maybe they will even win it. We will continue the cycle of hope, despair and hope again, which is the cycle of life. I will always follow my team. Maybe no longer from my seat at Ford Field, but will follow them nonetheless. We will always love our Lions.

APPENDIX A

Season recaps: 1976 - 1980

September 26th, 1976; a botched extra point with seconds left in the game results in a 10-9 loss to who else but the Vikings. Sound familiar? Nov. 14th, 1976; the Lions lose to the New Orleans Saints 17-16 even though we outplayed them significantly. Total yards; Detroit 455 - Saints 183. Landry throws for 310 yards, but 3 Lion fumbles, one resulting in a touchdown costs them the game. Nov. 25th, 1976 - Thanksgiving day; O.J. Simpson runs for 273 yards, the record at that time. I was at that game to see a man who would later kill 2 people break this record; I forgot he was found innocent. Sept. 25, 1977; the Lions lose to the Saints 23-19 even though they out gain them 429-92 yards offensively. Isn't that hard to do? These are the kind of performances Lion fans scratch their heads over. Dec. 11th, 1977; the Lions pull off the "I don't believe it" play for once beating Baltimore when Leonard Thompson blocks a punt for a touchdown with 14 seconds left, 13-10. Sept. 9, 1979; the Lions rally from a 21 point 4th quarter deficit to tie the game 24-24 against Washington. the Redskins kicker Mosley misses a 46 yard field goal with 8 seconds left in regulation; but you guessed it - the Lions are flagged for having 12 men on the field; re-kick from 41 yards; it's good - game over.

APPENDIX B

Season recaps: 1981 - 1985

On to the 1980's - the Billie Sims era. What a great running back; next to Barry Sanders, clearly the best back in my lifetime. A tragedy that his career was ended with a severe knee injury against who else? The Vikings of course. Sims debuts with a 100 yard plus game in a 41-20 win at the LA Rams. I remember watching that game and having a renewed sense of hope watching Sims run. After a 4-0 start, the Lions came out with a now infamous song "another one bites the dust", with Jimmy "spider man" Allen leading the way. That was the end of their 4 game streak and the end of their season. To this day, the song is played after particularly difficult loses. In game 5 that season, Atlanta beat us 43-28; the Falcons had 2 fumble returns for touchdowns and a blocked punt returned for a touchdown in the first half. The boys were probably a little tired from those nights in the recording studio. On to the famous ending Nov.27th, 1980; the Bears win the shortest overtime game in NFL history when Dave Williams returns the OT kickoff 95 yards for a touchdown - game over. This was after the Bears scored the tying touchdown as time

Sept. 13, 1981; the Lions lose the opener to San Diego 28-23; the Chargers score a TD with 56 seconds left in the game; a rally falls short when the Lions are intercepted at the San Diego 1 yard line as time expires. Sept. 20, 1981, our friends from Minnesota beat us on a field goal with 4 seconds left 26-24. A high point on Monday Night football Oct. 19th, 1981; Eric Hipple has a career game throwing for 4 touchdowns as the Lions beat the Bears 48-17. It is the highest point total for the Lions since 1957. A dark day that Lions fans remember well; Dec. 20.1981; the Lions lose to Tampa Bay on the final game of the season 20-17, costing them the Central title and a trip to the playoffs; our Lions had 3 drives inside the Bucs 20 yard line with no points; 2 interceptions and one on downs. "This team doesn't think it can win"! A new season, filled with hope - Sept. 19, 1982 - Sims runs for 119 yards and catches another 103 yards; only the 13th NFL player to do this. A 57 day player strike is followed by another memorable game; Nov. 25th, 1982; Lawrence Taylor returns an interception 97 yards in the 4th quarter to beat the Lions 13-6. That must mean that the Lions were really close to scoring the go ahead touchdown at the time - oops! Sept. 18, 1983 - another new season full of hope; maybe this will be the year for our Lions! "10 key players hampered by injuries", Sims breaks his hand during a 30-14 Atlanta win in game 2; that can't be good.

Back to the 1983 season; the Lions get their first ever overtime win 23-20 over the Packers on Nov. 20th, 1983. Dec. 5th, 1983; the Lions beat Minnesota 13-2; take that you bastards! Dec. 18th, 1983; the Lions beat Tampa 23-20 revenging the heartbreaking loss from 1 year earlier and winning the Central division title. These were the good times with Monty Clark when the Lions had a very good defense led by Doug English and Al Baker. On to the playoffs! This is getting exciting, don't you think? A day that will live in infamy in Lion history; Dec. 31st, 1983; the Lions out gain San Francisco 412-291; Gary Danielson drives the team down to the SF 25 yard line after the 49'ers go ahead with 1:23 left in the game. The famous picture of our coach praying to the football Gods as Eddie Murray approaches the 43 yard field goal attempt to go to the NFC Championship game. We all remember the results; the football Gods said "hell no", you must suffer once again - happy New Year"! Wide right, game over, wait until next year. Is that what that song means? "I left my torn out heart in San Francisco".

On to a new year; Sept. 9, 1984; the Lions beat the Falcons in overtime 27-24 on a 48 yard field goal by Eddie Murray; we could have used that in San Francisco 9 months earlier! Timing is everything. Sept. 23rd, 1984; Minnesota beats us in a typical Viking fashion, 29-28 - we don't even want to know the details, do we? The team has a memorable day Oct. 7th, 1984 when they lose to Denver 28-7 and have a record 10 turnovers (7 INT's and 3 fumbles); that's hard to do even for our Lions - but they are known for doing the impossible and the improbable. Another day that will always be remembered by Lion fans; Oct. 21st, 1984 - we beat the Vikings in Minnesota 16-14, but lose Billy Sims to a knee injury that will end his career. Of course, you would expect it to happen with the Vikings, wouldn't you?

Nov. 4th, 1984; a 23-23 tie with the Eagles; the Lions pull ahead with an 18 yard field goal (doesn't that mean we were on the 3 yard line and almost had a chance at a touchdown?) with 63 seconds to go, but our defense couldn't stop the Eagles from driving down the field and kicking a 40 yard field goal to tie the game with 3 seconds left. Don't worry, there is still overtime to win, right? Eddie Murray hits the upright in OT from 21 yards and the game ends up in a tie! 21 yards! Isn't an NFL kicker supposed to make that? That means of course that the drive stalled at the 4 yard line - darn, we were so close to a touchdown! I guess Murray never recovered from the 43 yard miss in San Francisco. The year ends with a unique performance by the Lions; they lose to the Bears on Dec. 16th, 1984 as the Bears sack the Lions 12 times. That is a lot of sacks - sounds like it should be an all time record, doesn't it?

Sept., 1985; the Darryl Rogers era begins - the coach who a few years later would have one of the famous, gutsy quotes of all time; "What's a guy gotta do around here to get fired?" Sept. 15th; Detroit beats Dallas 26-21 even though Dallas out gains us 554-200 yards but has 5 turnovers. Nov. 3rd, 1985; Vikings kick a field goal as time expires to win 16-13 - what's new? Nov. 24th, 1985; Tampa wins 19-16 in overtime, after the Lions were leading 16-6 until late in the game. Dec. 15th, 1985; the Packers win 26-23 by kicking a field goal as time expires. The Lions tied the game with 61 seconds left; go defense!

APPENDIX C

Season recaps: 1986 - 1990

Nov. 16th, 1986; the Lions beat the Eagles 13-11 and sack Cunningham 11 times - wouldn't that have been fun to see! Nov. 23rd, 1986' the Chuck Long era begins - he sets an NFL record by throwing his first pass for a 34 yard touchdown. It would be the highlight of his career. Nov. 27th, 1986; a thanksgiving game to remember - the Packers win the game by returning a punt 85 yards for a touchdown with 41 seconds left in the game. The Lions score 40 points; the most ever in a losing effort. Dec. 15th, 1986; the Bears win 16-13 on the final play of the game, kicking a 22 yard field goal.

Sept. 13, 1987; another new season - hope again; Vikings 34-19; the Lions led at halftime 16-10; Sept. 20, 1987 the Raiders win 27-7, once again the Lions led at the half 7-6. Sept. 27, 1987; a players strike with replacement players being used. Oct. 18, 1987; the Seahawks win 37-14 in front of 8,310 fans at the Silver dome. Oct. 25, 1987; the day before my 32nd birthday - the Lions surely had something special planned for me; they did! The Packers jump to a 24-0 lead, but the Lions come back to take a 33-31 lead with 2 minutes left. The Packers kick a 45 yard field goal to win the game 34-33; of course the Lions missed a 45 yard field goal of their own as time ran out - happy birthday to me! Dec. 20, 1987 the Vikings win 17-14 as Chuck Long throws an interception late in the game. Sept. 11, 1988; Rams beat the Lions 17-10; again Detroit had a 10-3 lead at halftime. Sept. 18, 1988; the Saints beat the Lions 22-14; a strange play in the game when the punter Arnold for Detroit attempts a pass that goes incomplete from the Lions 12 yard line - the receiver was not expecting the pass. Oct. 16, 1988; the Giants win 30-10 - again the Lions were leading at the half 10-7; Detroit had 113 yards of offense. Oct. 30, 1988; the Giants beat the Lions 13-10 in overtime - Detroit fumbles the first snap of the overtime, leading to the winning field goal. Nov. 6, 1988; Minnesota beats Detroit 44-17, out gaining the Lions 553-89 yards. Nov. 13, 1988; Darryl Rogers finally gets his answer to his question - being fired after Tampa beats the Lions 23-20 in overtime, with the Lions leading 20-17 with 52 seconds to play. A 52 yard field goal ties it and an overtime field goal wins it. Wayne Fontes takes over the team and leads the Lions to a 19-9 victory over the Packers on Nov. 20, 1988. Little did Lion fans know that Fontes would be the most successful coach we would have from 1957-2004. Nov. 24, 1988; the honeymoon is over Wayne - the Vikings welcome him as a head coach by crushing the Lions 23-0. Detroit never crossed the 50 yard line! The 60 yards and 3 first downs, the 3rd lowest production in team history. Dec. 11, 1988; the Bears beat the Lions 13-12 - Detroit goes up 12-10 on a late touchdown, but guess what? The Lions have the extra point blocked and Harbaugh drives Chicago down for the winning field goal of 32 yards. Maybe the league could give the Lions a break and just award them an extra point when they get a touchdown; they just seem to have a hard time with extra points!

A new year, a new player; Barry Sanders debuts Sept. 10, 1989 and takes his first carry for 18 yards. He ends his 1st game with 71 yards in 9 carries; but the Lions lose to the Cardinals 16-13 after a 33 yard field goal with 13 seconds left wins it for the Cardinals. Get used to it Barry! Sept. 17, 1989; the Giants win 24-14 even though the Lions led at halftime 7-3. Oct. 8, 1989; Minnesota wins 24-17; 3 Lions interceptions of which 2 are returned for touchdowns (15 and 90 yards). Oct. 15, 1989; the Lions beat Tampa when Rodney Peete scores a touchdown with 23 seconds left in the game - Eddie Murray kicked the extra point to win the game. It's interesting that the extra point was mentioned in the game summary. Oct. 22, 1989;

my birthday present from the Lions? A 20-7 loss to the Vikings - Detroit has 5 turnovers and are sacked 8 times. Oct. 29,1989; the Packers beat Detroit 23-20 in overtime. The Lions fumble in Packer territory with less than a minute left in regulation, and then throw an interception on the 1st play in overtime. Sanders outstanding performance of 180 yards on 30 carries is wasted. Nov. 5, 1989; Houston wins 35-31 - Detroit had a halftime lead 17-14. Detroit threatens in the last minute, but throws an interception to end the game. Dec. 24, 1989; Detroit beats Atlanta 31-24 - we all remember this last game of the decade, as Barry Sanders rushes for 158 yards and 3 touchdowns, but refuses Wayne Fontes and teammates urging him to return and win the rushing title. Sanders said the game was in hand, and the title didn't mean much to him. I remember being disappointed when he did that. Lion fans don't often get to say one of their players was the best in the league.

Sept. 9, 1990; a new season, a new decade, a new result? Nope, Tampa wins 38-21; the Lions have 6 turnovers and are sacked 6 times. Sept. 23, 1990; again Tampa 23-20 on a last minute touchdown. Sept. 30, 1990; Green Bay 24-21 on a TD with less than a minute to play - a chance to tie ends when Eddie Murray misses a 44 yard field goal attempt. Oct. 7, 1990; the Lions pull off a come back after being down 20-10 at the half to Minnesota and win 34-27; we aren't used to the comeback victory. Oct. 28, 1990; a great birthday present for me - Lions beat the Saints 27-10 forcing 8 turnovers. Shouldn't you score more than 27 when you get 8 turnovers? Nov. 4, 1990; the Redskins win 41-38 in overtime - Detroit led 35-14 in the 3rd; Washington gains 674 yards. Nov. 11, 1990; the Andre Ware era begins! Lions lose 17-7. Dec. 2, 1990; the Bears win 23-17 in overtime - Chicago kicks a field goal with 33 seconds left to force OT; Eddie Murray misses a 35 yard field goal in OT for the win. Dec. 16, 1990; Lions beat the Bears 38-21 - Detroit has 411 yards of offense, the most in 5 years! Is it that hard to get over 400 yards? Dec. 22, 1990; a great and unusual come back win for Detroit in -35 degree wind chill at Green Bay - Detroit scores 14 in the 4th and bounces the Packers out of the playoffs. Dec. 30, 1990; Seattle 30-10 over Detroit, but Barry Sanders wins the rushing title with 23 yards and beats out Thurman Thomas by 7 yards (1,304 yards).

APPENDIX D

Season recaps: 1991 - 1995

Sept. 15, 1991; the best year the Lions would have in the 34 years since 1970 - Detroit 17-13 over Miami; the Lions have a 4 play goal line stance with under 5 minutes left in the game to stop Marino from the 3 yard line for the win. Oct. 6, 1991; Detroit beats the Vikings with 3 4th quarter touchdowns 24-20, as Sanders runs 15 yards for the winning score with 46 seconds left in the game - it's looking like a special season! Oct. 27, 1991; a 34-10 win over Dallas - Peete injures his Achilles and is replaced by Eric Kramer. Nov. 3, 1991; the Bears win 20-10 in -8 wind chill - Detroit was up 10-3 at halftime; Lions are 2-13 on 3rd down. Nov. 24, 1991; Sanders runs for 4 touchdowns and gains 220 yards in win over the Vikings. Dec. 8, 1991; the Lions go 8-0 at home - their 1st undefeated home season since 1962; with a 34-20 win over the Jets - it is the 5th 10 win season in Lion history (that's all!). Dec. 15, 1991; the Lions beat the Packers 21-17 in -18 wind chill - Mel Grey runs a punt back 78 yards for the winning touchdown in the 4th. Dec. 22, 1991; Buffalo scores a last minute touchdown to force overtime, but the Lions Eddie Murray wins it in OT with a 21 yard field goal, snapping the Bills 17 home game winning streak. It is the first 12 win season in Lion history. On to the only playoff win I have witnessed in my lifetime! Detroit 38-6 over the Cowboys on Jan. 5, 1992; Kramer is brilliant going 29-38 for 341 yards and 3 touchdowns - Herman Moore catches his first touchdown pass. On to the NFC championship game - we are 1 game away from the super bowl; could it be true? No! Washington 41-10; the dream is over - we were only down 17-10 at the half. It was a fantastic season though.

Sept. 6, 1992; Bears 27-24 - the Lions take the lead on an 80 yard drive and touchdown with 1:12 left; a 74 yard drive by Harbaugh results in the winning touchdown with 1 second left! We were so close. Sept. 20, 1992; Washington 13-10 - the Lions miss a 49 yard field goal as time runs out. Sept. 27, 1992; Tampa Bay 27-23 - Mel Grey returns a kick 89 yards for a TD with 5:43 left. Bucs 80 yard TD drive to re-take the lead. Lions go 79 yards in 42 seconds but fall short at the 3 yard line as time expires. Darn, we were so close again! Nov. 8, 1992; Cowboys 37-3 - worse home loss for the Lions since 1964; Mel Grey sets a Lion record with 8 kickoff returns! Does that mean the other team scored a lot? Nov. 15, 1992; the Lions give the Steelers a "scare", but lose 17-14; Disaster strikes late in the 4th with the Lions up 14-10 - Detroit fumbles deep in their own zone and it is returned to the Lion 3 yard line to set up the winning touchdown. The game ends on the Steelers 19 yard line after a great catch by Perriman. Darn, we were so close again! Nov. 26, 1992; Houston 24-21 - the Oilers drive for the winning touchdown with less than 3 minutes left in the game. Is this fair? Dec. 20, 1992; The Lions win 16-3 over the Bears - Ware throws for 290 yards - why didn't he ever make it? Sept. 12, 1993; the Lions beat New England 19-16 in overtime - Bledsoe throws a TD pass with 12 seconds left to tie it, but Hanson wins it in OT with a 38 yard field goal. Sept. 19, 1993; the Saints win 14-3 - the Lions get 3 first downs and gain 29 yards in the second half. Is this why Ware never made it? Oct. 3, 1993; Tampa 27-10 - Sanders 107 yards in the first half; 23 in the second half (adjustments!) - In the 1st drive of the game, the Lions go 80 yards on 5 plays, they looked like "world beaters". Oct. 17, 1993; the Lions beat Seattle 30-10 - rookie QB Rick Mire had problems (3 INT's and 3 sacks); today he is a Lion! Oct, 24, 1993; happy 38th birthday from the Lions - they beat the Rams 16-13 breaking an 11 game west cost losing streak. This time, the Rams score a TD with 1:52 left, but miss the extra point (where did they learn how to do that?) - Detroit kicks a winning FG as time runs out. Oct. 31, 1993; the Lions have a come from behind win 30-27 after being down 27-13 after 3 quarters; Detroit scores with 40 seconds left for the victory. Nov. 7, 1993; Detroit beats Tampa 23-0 - Sanders runs for 187 yards; their 7-2 record is the best start for the Lions since 1962. Hard to believe we have not been 7-2 in 31 years, isn't it? Nov. 25, 1993; Bears 10-6 - Sanders injures his knee - Detroit has 4 turnovers. Dec. 5, 1993; Vikings 13-0 - they get 7 sacks and 5 interceptions. Dec. 19, 1993; San Francisco 55-17 - the 49'ers have no punts and gain 565 yards - they're pretty good!. Jan. 2, 1994; the Lions beat the Packers 30-20 to win the Central title! Green Bay had 5 turnovers. Jan. 8, 1994; hey, didn't we just play the Packers? This time it's in the playoffs; we all remember this one - we lose a "heartbreaker" (has that ever happened before?) 28-24 to Green Bay; Sanders returns and runs for 169 yards - this game would see a 101 yard TD on an interception return by the Packers; a 40 yard TD pass to a wide open Sterling Sharpe (did someone miss their coverage perhaps?) with 55 seconds left ends the season in typical depressing fashion. There's always next year, right?

Back to our Lions; I have now reviewed the summaries of 384 games since 1970. I think I'm dizzy! So many of the tortured, "I don't believe it" memories I recalled. Only 10 years to go. Sept. 4, 1994; Lions beat Atlanta 31-28 in OT - Mitchell TD pass to Anthony Carter with 30 secs left to tie. Hanson kicks a 37 yard FG for the OT win. Sept. 11, 1194; Vikings 10-3; Lions get 2 first downs and 29 yards in the first half - hold Minnesota to one 1st down and 59 yards in the second half. Sept. 19, 1994; Lions beat Dallas 20-17 in OT on Monday night - Sanders runs for 194; Detroit has 2 FG's blocked at the end of regulation and start of OT, but they prevail on a 44 yard FG with 32 seconds left in OT; one of the great wins of all time! Oct. 30, 1994; Lions 28-25 over the Giants in OT - we set an NFL record by being the only team to ever win 3 OT games in a season. Nov. 6, 1994; Packers 38-30 - 4 first half turnovers by Detroit; Craig rallies the Lions back from 38-14 starting the fourth, but falls short on downs at the Green Bay 15 yard line as time runs out. Nov. 1994; Detroit beats Tampa 14-9 - Sanders runs for 237; 200 in the 2nd half; wow! Nov. 20, 1994; the Bears win holding the ball an amazing 44:12. Dec. 10, 1994; the Lions beat the Jets 18-7 as Chris Speilman sets the record for most tackles by a Lion with 166. Now that was a pure athlete who won the hearts and respect of Lion fans. I never understood why he left the team a few years before an injury ended his career. Dec. 17, 1994; Detroit beats the hated Vikings 41-19 - take that evil empire! Barry Sanders has his 6th run of 60 yards or more this season; can you imagine that? It's playoff time, are you excited? Packers 16-12 as Sanders is held to -1 yard on 13 carries (how could that be?); Detroit gained 58 yards and 2 first downs in the opening half - Herman Moore catches a pass for what appears to be a go ahead touchdown, but is ruled out of the end zone. Darn, we were so close. Wait until next year?

Sept. 5, 1995; Steelers 23-20 - a 31 yd field goal as time runs out wins it after Detroit tied the score with 3 minutes left; the Lions had 4 interceptions. Sept. 17, 1995; Arizona 20-17 as the Cardinals score 14 points in the 4th to overcome a 17-6 Lion lead. Detroit has 15 penalties and loses 2 fumbles by Sanders - the Lions record 7 sacks. Sept. 25, 1995; Detroit 27-24 over the 49'ers - who hit the upright on a 40 yard field goal attempt missing as time runs out. Oct. 22, 1995; time for my birthday present! Redskins 36-30 in overtime as Washington beats Detroit for the 17th time in a row; isn't that hard to do? The Lions were intercepted 4 times, the final one in OT for a touchdown and the Redskin win. Washington kicked a field goal as time expired to force overtime. The Redskins streak reminds you of the Viking streak from the 70's. Nov. 12, 1995; Detroit 27-24 over Tampa - Wayne Fontes becomes the coach with the most wins in Lions history with number 56 (breaks George Wilson's 55 wins); Isn't that amazing, that since 1934 no coach had ever won more than 55 games before today? Nov. 23, 1995; Lions 44-38 over Minnesota - Scott Mitchell sets a new Lion record by passing for 410 yards (breaking Bobby Lanes 374 yards in 1950).Dec. 10, 1995; Detroit 24-17 over the Oilers - Mitchell breaks the record by Bobby Lane of 26 touchdown passes in a season. Dec. 17, 1995; Lions 44-0 over Jacksonville - Moore and Perriman both catch over 100 passes each; the 1st time ever in NFL history. Dec. 23, 1995; Lions 37-10 over Tampa - the 1st 7 game winning streak since 1962 for Detroit. On to the playoffs with our 7 game winning streak; we are unstoppable right? Wrong. Eagles 58-37 in the highest scoring playoff game in history. A total collapse when it counts! 7 Lion turnovers including 6 interceptions. Philadelphia was up 51-7 as Rodney Peete (hey, wasn't he on our team? that's not fair, is it?) goes 17-25, for 270 yards and 3 touchdowns. Maybe he wanted to send a message to Detroit for trading him. It was Detroit's 3rd straight playoff appearance and third straight exit in the first round. When it counts the most...happy new years from your Lions!

APPENDIX E

Season recaps: 1996 - 2000

Sept. 1, 1996; a "gut wrenching" 17-13 loss to the Vikings - Lions have 5 turnovers; Herman Moore becomes the all time touchdown leader for Detroit with 36 (that doesn't seem like very many, does it?) - Mitchell's 4th interception stalls the final drive at the Viking 11 yard line. Oct. 27, 1996; happy birthday! Giants 35-7 with 2 interception returns for touchdowns. Nov. 17, 1996; Detroit 17-16 over Seattle - the Seahawks miss a 42 yard field goal as time expires (it can happen to anyone!). Nov. 24, 1996; Bears 31-14 - Sanders record 8th 1000 yard season in a row; 1st NFL player to ever achieve this in 8 consecutive seasons. Nov. 28, 1996; Chiefs win 28-24 - Detroit leads 24-21 and KC drives the final 8 minutes before scoring the winning touchdown. Dec. 8, 1996; Vikings 24-22 - Sanders scores a late touchdown, but the Lions miss the 2 point conversion to tie. Dec. 23, 1996; a disappointing season ends with a 49'er win 24-14; like usual, the only good news was Sanders running for 175 yards and his 3rd rushing title. Wait until next year?

Aug. 31, 1997, the "Bobby Ross era" begins with a 28-14 win over Atlanta. Oct. 5, 1997; Buffalo 22-13 - Sanders is tackled for a safety with 2 minutes left when it was 13-13. Oct. 12, 1997; Detroit 27-9 over Tampa - Sanders runs for 215 yards and 2 TD's; he becomes the 1st player in NFL history to have 2 runs for 80 yards in the same game. Oct. 19, 1997; an early birthday present - Giants 26-20 in overtime; the Lions score a TD with 2 minutes left, but the Giants win the coin toss for OT and throw a 68 yard TD on the 3rd play of overtime - game over! Nov. 2, 1997; Packers 20-10 - 14-10 Packers at the half; Detroit is scoreless in the 2nd half as the Packers pick off 4 Lion passes for INT's. Nov. 9, 1997; Redskins 30-7 winning their 16th straight over Detroit (unbelievable!) - Washington had the ball for 40 minutes; Sanders moves past Dorsett for 3rd all time rushing. Nov. 23, 1997; Lions 32-10 over the Colts - Sanders 3rd run of 80 plus yards in the season; another NFL record! Nov. 27, 1997; Lions 55-20 over the Bears - the most ever points in a regular season game for Detroit; the most points ever given up by a Bears team - Sanders moves into 2nd place all time rushing ahead of Eric Dickerson (13,319 yards); Jason Hanson kicks his 23rd straight field goal, also a team record. Dec. 7, 1997; a "heart breaking" loss to Miami 33-30 - the Lions have 5 turnovers; after scoring a TD, Detroit misses the extra point trailing 23-22 - the Lions tie the game on a 96 yard drive and 2 point conversion; with 1:54 left in the game, Miami drives 54 yards and kicks the winning field goal. How many of these can we take? I guess as many as the Lions give us! Dec. 14, 1997; Detroit 14-13 over the Vikings - Mitchell leads the team on a 72 yard drive and TD in the final 2 minutes for the win. Herman Moore has his 3rd consecutive 100 catch season (only Jerry Rice had done it); Sanders runs for his 13th straight 100 yard plus game setting another NFL record. The guy is simply amazing, and by far the most exciting Lion I have ever seen. Dec. 21, 1997; the Lions beat the Jets 13-10 - Sanders becomes the 3rd player to ever rush for over 2000 yards; the Jets end the game on a Lion INT of a half back option pass - most memorable in this game was the near tragedy with linebacker Reggie Brown after he stopped breathing on the field after a collision; I will never forget the feeling in the Silver dome - many of us thought this young man had died. Is it possible that I am in the stands watching a 2nd NFL player die? I never thought it would be possible after the sad day with Chuck Hughes. Thank god Reggie Brown would be o.k., even though his NFL career ended that day. Dec. 28, 1997; the playoffs - how exciting, right? Wrong! the Lions 4th playoff appearance in the past 5 years ends the same way they all have - Tampa 20-10.

Sept. 6, 1998; a new season - new hope; Packers 38-19 - Fair has a 101 yard kick return for a TD, but the Packers match it on the next play with a 100 yard return of their own - the 4th time in history this has occurred; Sanders 14 game streak of 100 yards rushing is snapped as he runs for 70 yards. Sept. 13, 1998; the Bengal's beat Detroit 34-28 in OT in "heart wrenching" fashion - have we heard this term before? Sanders TD with 1:52 left to tie - Spindler blocks a 48 yard field goal to force overtime; A 58 yard interception return for a TD ends the game in OT. Oct. 4, 1998; Bears 31-27; Detroit led 27-10 starting the 4th - Chicago had 5 fumbles (aren't you supposed to win when you get five turnovers?); Batch throws his first TD pass 98 yards to Morton - we get to the Bears 15 yard line, but holding brings it back ending the Lion chances. Oct. 15, 1998; Detroit 27-20 over the Packers - Batch 11 straight completions, the youngest QB to achieve this since 1992 - his 84.2 rating was the highest for a rookie since 1960. Sanders 25th time running for 150 yards; he has his 15th run of his career of 50 yards plus - both NFL records. Oct. 25, 1998; I can't wait to see what the Lions give me for my birthday present this year! Vikings 34-13; Lions led 13-10 at halftime - doesn't that mean that we were shut out in the second half? How come the games have to last so long? Nov. 1, 1998; Cardinals 17-15; wasn't this the game with the controversial 2 point conversion try? Detroit had 6 turnovers. Nov. 8, 1998; Eagles 10-9; this game represents many of the worst frustrations fans have faced over the years with the Lions. The winning field goal is good even though it hit Spindlers forearm and went through; the final drive for the Lions stalls at the 39 yard line, after 4 Detroit penalties (2 holding, 1 false start and an illegal pass) - the 58 yard attempt by Hanson is no good - game over! The "silver lining in the disappointing loss is Sanders reaching 1000 yards for the 10th straight year. I'm sure I would have "snapped" many years before I did if it wasn't for Barry Sanders. Nov. 26, 1998; Detroit 19-16 over the Steelers in OT; the Steelers tied it as time ran out to force OT - Detroit wins the coin toss, but Bettis would later say he called the correct tails and the ref. didn't hear him; strange things happen when the Lions are involved; Detroit kicks a FG to win in OT. Dec. 14, 1998; 49'ers 35-13 Monday night - San Fran rushes for

328 yards. Dec. 20, 1998; Atlanta 24-17; the Lions held a 17-10 lead starting the 4th (why can't the game be shorter?) - Moore becomes the fastest receiver to 600 receptions (118 games). Does this mean we are not going to the super bowl? See you guys next year!

Sept. 12, 1999; Detroit 28-20 over Seattle - the 1st opening road win since 1986; the Lions led 25-7 at the half. Sept. 19, 1999; Lions 23-15 over the Packers - it's the 1st opening day sellout at home since 1975. Is that possible? Oct. 10, 1999; San Diego 20-10 - it was 10-10 at the half; Detroit is sacked 6 times and has 2 turnovers - a 42 yard TD return of a fumble in the 4th is the difference. Oct. 17, 1999; Detroit 25-23 over the Vikings - the Lions led 19-0 at the half; is it me or is there a pattern of the Lions playing poorly in the second half? Frerotte drives 43 yards in final 1:40 to set up Hanson's winning field goal with 7 seconds left - it was Hanson's 6th FG of the day. Oct. 24, 1999; the boys come through for my birthday, beating Carolina 24-9; the Lion defense holds the Panthers to 3 FG's with 5 possessions inside the Lion 5 yard line - now there is some defense! Nov. 7, 1999; Detroit beats the Rams 31-27; Frerotte's TD pass with 28 seconds left, which was set up by a 4th and 26 first down - Rice intercepts Warner to end it. Nov. 14, 1999; Arizona wins 23-19; the infamous 2 point controversy! Detroit comes back from 23-7 - Frerotte throws for 375 yards; the 1st 2 point try comes at 23-13 - at 23-19, another 2 point try fails . Boss Ross was 2nd guessed for not taking the point and pulling to within a field goal; the Lions final drive stalls at the Cardinal 10 yard line as TRO (time runs out). Nov. 21, 1999; Packers 26-17; Lions led at the half 17-12 (why so many poor 2nd half performances - I say it's coaching). Nov. 25, 1999; Detroit 21-17 over Tampa - the Lions led 21-0 late in the first half; we have never had the killer instinct to put teams away when they are down. Dec. 5, 1999; Detroit 33-17 over the Redskins - breaking a 16 game losing streak to Washington! Hanson kicks 4 field goals for the 10th time in his career, 2 were from 50 plus yards; he becomes only the second kicker in NFL history to kick 2 50 yard FG's in a game in 2 different games. Although this is a great accomplishment, and Hanson a fantastic kicker, it means the Lions have problems scoring touchdowns, doesn't it? Dec. 12, 1999; a "gut wrenching" 23-16 loss to Tampa - how many times have we used the term "gut wrenching"? I think the term sums up the past 47 years! Detroit leads this one 10-7 at the half and 16-9 early in the 4th; the Lions run a kickoff back to the Tampa 14 yard line - oops! an illegal block takes it away; "I don't coach them to play that way." Dec. 25, 1999; Merry Christmas - Denver 17-7; the Lions rush for 32 yards (where is Barry Sanders? Oh I forgot, he snapped and couldn't take it anymore also, retiring from football this past training camp! We miss you Barry. Jan. 2, 2000; we move to a new century! This will surely inspire our Lions. What? Vikings 24-17; their 4th loss in a row even though they clinched their 6th playoff birth in the 1990's (hey, they won 1 of them). Every team hopes for a 4 game losing streak going into the playoffs - great for momentum! Washington 27-14; Rice has a 94 yard TD return on a blocked field goal. Is this the start of another 16 game losing streak to the Redskins?

Sept. 3, 2000; Lions 14-10 over Saints - 439 total yards for both teams; 95 yard TD return by Desmond Howard - Lions botched the snap on a 29 yard field goal ("I don't coach em that way"); Saints get to the Lions 29 as time runs out. Sept. 10, 2000; Lions 15-10 over Redskins - 5 Hanson field goals; 4 interceptions for Detroit - Fair INT. with 49 seconds left at the Lion 20 to seal the win. Sept. 24, 2000; Detroit 21-14 over Chicago - 1st time since 1980 the Lions win their 1st 2 on the road (that's pretty sad, isn't it?); 5 turnovers by the Bears - Lions 14-0 at half, but the Bears tie 14-14; Lions win on a 91 yard drive taking 8:37 for a TD. Oct. 8, 2000; Lions 31-24 over Packers - Detroit led 24-6 at half (can't put teams away!); Green Bay has 5 turnovers - 2 late INT's seal it for Detroit. Oct. 19, 2000; Lions 28-14 over Tampa - 11-11 at the half (1st time in NFL history); 4 Tampa turnovers. Oct. 29, 2000; a belated birthday present - Colts 30-18 over Detroit; Indianapolis has 5 turnovers, but leads at the half 23-0 (is that possible?) Nov. 5, 2000; Miami 23-8 over the Lions - Dolphins jump off to a 14-0 lead early after recovering an on side kick after their opening TD; 14-0 before Detroit touches the ball (bad start to a game) - Batch leaves the game with a concussion; Ross quits after this one. Nov. 12, 2000; the Moeller era begins with a 13-10 win over the Falcons - a Hanson 44 yard field goal with 30 seconds left wins it. Nov. 19, 2000; Lions 31-21 over the Giants - Detroit led

28-0 early in the 3rd; Westbrook has a 101 yard INT for TD. Dec. 10, 2000; Packers 26-13 - 5 Lion turnovers; Detroit gets back to 12-10 down, but a 6 play 80 yard drive gives the Packers a 19-10 lead (how many times have the Lions scored big TD"S to get back in a game, just to have the defense let up a TD on the very next drive?). Dec. 17, 2000; Lions beat the Jets 10-7 when Hardings recovers a Stuart fumble in the end zone for their only TD - the Jets miss a 36 yard field goal with 12 seconds left to end it. Dec. 24, 2000; the game that will be remembered forever! Lions need a win to go to the playoffs, and lose to the Bears 23-20 when Edinger kicks a 54 yard field goal with 2 seconds left (ooch!); It was another "gut wrenching" loss. Detroit had the 10-0 lead in this one - with 2 minutes left Detroit recovers a Bear fumble in Chicago territory, but Stony Case (in for Batch who left with a rib injury) could not move the team - Detroit settles for a 26 yard field goal to tie; Case fumbles on the last drive, to set up the winning kick. Mr. Ford might "snap" over this one!

APPENDIX F

Season recaps: 2001 - 2003

Sept. 23, 2001; Marty Mornhinweg is in for a rough two years – Cleveland 24-14; Detmer throws 7 interceptions and the Lions have 15 penalties. Oct. 8, 2001; Rams 35-0; Oct. 14, 2001; Vikings 31-26 – the Lions come back from 31-6 down; they get to the Viking 20 yard line as time runs out. Oct. 21,2001; Titans 27-24 – Detroit ties with 1:18 left, but a field goal with 10 seconds left wins it for Tennessee; I guess the defense couldn't hold! Oct. 28, 2001; Bengal's 31-27 – 1st offensive play for Cincinnati is a 96 yard TD run by Dillion; not a good start. Nov. 11,2001; Tampa 20-17 – it was another "heartbreaking loss" (have we heard this term before?); Detroit tied the game 17-17 with 1:54 left, but you guessed it – the defense can't hold; a 35 yard field goal with 4 seconds left ends it. Nov. 18, 2001; Arizona scores 24 in the 4th to win – Batch is 36-62 for 436 yards; both Lion records. Nov. 22, 2001; the Lions "nearly" pull off a 4th quarter 16 point deficit but fall 29-27 to the Packers – a Lion TD and recovered on side kick with 1:17 left, but the 2 point conversion is missed. Dec. 2, 2001; the Bears win when Hanson misses a 40 yard field goal with 24 seconds left for the tie. Dec. 9, 2001, after an 0-12 start, the Lions lose another "heartbreaker" to Tampa 15-12. Tampa scores a TD with 45 seconds left for the win; Mike McMahon's 1st start. Dec. 16, 2001; Lions 1st win of the season! They beat the Vikings (take that you bastards!) and keep Minnesota out of the playoffs. Dec. 23, 2001; Steelers 40-7 – Sloan catches his 6th TD pass of the year (ties him with Charlie Sanders for most TD's in a year for a tight end). That's not very many to be a record, is it? Jan. 6, 2002 – thank god this season is over; if we feel that way, you can imagine how the players feel! Lions 15-10 over Dallas; the last game at the Silver dome – Morton catches his 35th TD pass, tying him for 2nd most ever by a Lion receiver. That's not very many over a career, is it?

Sept. 22, 2002; another season, another lose; Packers 37-31 for the 1st game at Ford Field – Harrington's heroics falls short as a pass is dropped in the final seconds. Oct. 13, 2002; Vikings 31-24 – Minnesota scores 21 in the 2nd half for the win. Oct. 20, 2002; Lions 23-20 over the Bears – the headline reads, "Stuart shows Lions are not so cowardly." I knew this team had something in common with The Wizard and Oz! Nov. 3, 2002; Lions 9-7 over the Cowboys – Detroit kicks a winning field goal with 48 seconds left. Nov. 24, 2002; a famous day in Lion history – Marty takes the wind at Chicago in overtime; Detroit never touches the ball – Bears 20-17. Dec. 15, 2002; Tampa 23-20 – the "Lions slept early", but come back to make it close; Harrington is being treated for an irregular heart beat. Dec. 29, 2002; Vikings 38-36 – a McMahon TD pass with 13 seconds left, but the 2 point conversion is no good; darn, they were so close again! The 2 point conversion failed "and the heart of the Lions were sunk." Mornhinweg says "the team is primed to make a run, but it's still a handful of players away." The bar is high! He might be in trouble.

Sept. 7, 2003; Lions 42-24 over the Cardinals – the "Mouch" era begins on a high note; don't get too excited dedicating the game ball to Mr. Ford after the game – the leading rusher for the Lions' gets 44 yards, the leading receiver gets 38 yards. It was the best rookie receiver performance since 1947 – Boldin catches for 217 yards; "Mariucci says it was "an emotional day." There will be more to come! Sept. 14, 2003; Packers 31-6 – a 64 TD run on the second play of the game by Green Bay. Sept. 28, 2003; Denver 20-16 over the Lions – the Lions lose their 18th straight road game; Detroit scores the apparent game tying touchdown in the 4th, but misses the point after due to a bad snap (have we heard this one before?); Denver wins on a 41 yard field goal with 3:13 left – guess we didn't do well on the last drive. Oct. 5, 2003; 49'ers 24-17 – Detroit comes back from 17-0. Oct. 19, 2003; Cowboys 38-7 over Detroit – the Lions open the scoring on a 69 yard TD fumble return by Bly; I guess they didn't do too well after that! Oct. 26, 2003; my birthday! Bears 24-16 over the Lions – Lions score with 53 seconds left and appear to recover the on side kick; darn, there is a penalty for an illegal touch before ten yards – we were so close. Do you think they would have scored, got a 2 point conversion, and won in overtime? Maybe not. Nov. 9, 2003; Detroit 12-10 over the Bears – Hanson kicks 4 field goals; Detroit rushes for 12 yards – our receiver Swinton leads the team in rushing with 9 yards. Nov. 23, 2003; Vikings 24-14 – Minnesota scores 17 points in a 45 second span in the 4th; that can't be good. Nov. 27, 2003; Lions 22-14 over the Packers – it's so sad that the Lion web site says "at 4-8, they have surpassed their win victory totals each of the past 2 seasons." Bly intercepted 2 and forced a fumble. Dec. 14, 2003; the Chiefs win 45-17 – KC scores on 7 of their first 8 possessions and have a total of 521 yards. The Lions tie the all time NFL record for consecutive road loses with their 23rd straight. See, we are special! Dec. 21, 2003; a proud day in Lion history; the record 24th loss in a row on the road – Detroit has 8 1st downs and 106 yards of offense. Dec. 28, 2003; Lions beat the Rams 30-20 – Mariucci tells the team early in the week "just put one game together"; now it is clear why he makes 5 million a year. It was the 1st time they scored over 23 points since the opening game against Arizona. Bly becomes the first Lion to start the Pro Bowl at corner since 1977. The website concludes by saying "the Lions carved out a program changing 30-20 win in the last game against the Rams – shunning the Rams quest for home field advantage throughout the playoffs." Program changing? Let's see!

Source: www.DetroitLions.com

Printed in the United States
62284LVS00006B/1-213